CREATE A CARD

with stickers, stencils and stamps

STEPHANIE WEIGHTMAN

NEW
HOLLAND

This edition first published in 2006
First published in 2005 by
New Holland Publishers (UK) Ltd
London • Cape Town • Sydney • Auckland

Garfield House
86–88 Edgware Road
London W2 2EA
www.newhollandpublishers.com

80 McKenzie Street
Cape Town 8001
South Africa

Level 1, Unit 4
14 Aquatic Drive
Frenchs Forest, NSW 2086
Australia

218 Lake Road
Northcote
Auckland
New Zealand

10 9 8 7 6 5 4 3 2 1

ISBN 1 84537 579 3

Senior Editor: Corinne Masciocchi
Designer: Peter Crump
Photographer: Shona Wood
Editorial Director: Rosemary Wilkinson
Production: Hazel Kirkman

Reproduction by Pica Digital PTE Ltd, Singapore
Printed and bound by Times Offset (M) Sdn. Bhd., Malaysia

This book I dedicate to my sister Zoë, my
business partner and best friend.

Acknowledgements

Firstly, I'd like to thank you, the reader –
beginners and experienced card makers
alike – as without you and the
extraordinary passion that card makers
exude, books like this would only ever be
a dream.

There are so many people I need to
thank: the team at New Holland; special
thanks go to Corinne and Clare for their
unfailing patience, Shona for her
unrivalled talent, and to Rosemary for
giving me the opportunity to write
another book. I also have to say a huge
thank you to my team at work, especially
Debbie and Zoë, whom even through late
nights and a busy year pulled out all the
stops to help. If anyone has been missed
off I can only say please forgive me for
being so absorbed in such an exciting
book. Thank you everyone.

CREATE A CARD

with stickers and stamps

12.

18.

contents

Introduction

Some of my first childhood memories are of gluing and sticking down pieces of paper. As an adult, making cards allows me to indulge this memory and put it to good use. Like all crafts, card making is a therapeutic but nevertheless addictive hobby. If it is something you have never tried I urge you to have a go. It is so simple to make professional-looking cards that, together with a few simple instructions and top tips, you will be amazed at just how easy and rewarding it is.

Creating hand-made cards has in recent years become very fashionable, so much so that you will find many card and gift shops selling 'hand-finished' greeting cards. How many times have you walked out of a card shop thinking 'I could make that card?' I hope this book inspires you to do just that. Using a multitude of products and techniques, there are over 35 card-making projects for both beginners and the more advanced crafters to make.

The book is divided into three main chapters that include the techniques and a selection of beautiful projects for stickers, stencils and stamps.

Stickers are a great starting point: they are simple to use, yet create stunning effects. They are often bought ready-made or designed to simply sit on the front of a card, but you can also make your own stickers at home so there are almost no limits to what you can design or achieve!

Stencils were traditionally made from mylar plastic or oiled manila card and were – and still are – used with stencil creams, stencil paints or decorative chalks applied to the stencil and onto the chosen support. Stencils now come in flexible plastic with a self-adhesive surface that bonds tightly to the support, allowing you to use any number of colouring implements without any bleeding. These are very versatile as they are washable and therefore reusable. Stencils also come in a large number of metals to create raised paper impressions such as those done with dry embossing or to use as templates to cut design patterns.

Stamping is a card-making craft that has been around for a number of years but if you have never tried it before you will find simple projects to get you started and if you are an experienced stamper you will find new ideas and inspiration.

There is something for everyone so I hope you enjoy making the various card projects in this book as much as sending them to your loved ones.

Stephanie Weightman

Tools and materials

Making greeting cards can be as quick and easy or as intricate as you choose to make it. You can start with a simple set of tools and materials such as a pair of good quality scissors and a selection of interesting coloured papers. As you become more involved, you may like to invest in a large carry case or box to store all your craft products so that they are close to hand. Below are a selection of tools and materials that are useful for card making.

Cards and glues, rulers and scissors

1 card stock there is a wide range of different cards and papers on the market. Commercially made papers come in sizes ranging from A1 to A4. Most of the cards in this book use a weight of approximately 280 to 330 gsm (grams per square meter) for the main card stock.

2 glue stick multi-purpose glue used mainly for layering backing cards.

3 adhesive paste used to stick down 3-D embellishments or as a sticky layer to sprinkle with glitter.

4 glue dots come in a selection of sizes. Simply take the card or embellishment to the glue dot, remove the dot from the backing sheet and position in place.

5 3-D foam glue pads used for 3-D decoupage and to raise card and paper from the surface it is mounted on. The pads are usually about 4 mm (¹/4 in) thick with adhesive on both sides.

6 micro glue dots usually come on an A6 sheet. Simply press the surface you want to stick down to the glue dots and peel back: the dots will stick to the surface. Ideal for use on vellum as these small dots are almost invisible.

7 spray adhesive available in repositionable or permanent varieties. The former is useful when you are planning a card and are not ready to secure everything permanently in place. Sprays are usually solvent-based so you will need to work in a well-ventilated area.

8 low tack masking tape always a handy craft material to have in your box. Great for holding down stencils and especially useful when securing a design before cutting with a craft knife.

9 metal ruler invest in a metal ruler for cutting and scoring cards.

10 plastic ruler a clear plastic ruler is good for lining up and measuring at the same time.

11 decorative edge scissors great for creating border effects. Draw a line with a pencil and ruler and use it as a guide when cutting with the scissors.

Decorative papers and stickers

1 outline stickers commonly referred to as peel-offs, they are inexpensive and available in a number of designs. They are easy to use and make quick and colourful cards.

2 mulberry paper semi-opaque hand-made paper made from mulberry leaves and silk strands. It can be expensive so use in small quantities.

3 talcum powder applied to the back of pre-made stickers to prevent unwanted areas of glue from sticking to card stock.

4 vellum sheer paper with a subtle translucent finish, available in a wide range of colours.

5 printed vellum sheer paper printed with a wide range of designs and colours. Look out for co-ordinating plain and patterned paper ranges.

6 metallic and holographic decorative cards these cards give a striking look to hand-made cards. Available in a good range of colours and a variety of eye-catching patterns.

7 rubdown stickers rub over the sticker with a lolly stick through the protective film onto your chosen surface. Suitable for use on paper and wooden and glass surfaces.

8 holographic outline stickers second generation of outline stickers or peels-offs designed to create simple but effective greeting cards.

9 micro bead stickers pre-made stickers coated with micro beads to create a textured finish.

10 pre-finished stickers designed to make card making simple, just peel and stick.

Pens, pencils and paints

1 stencil paints a good painting medium to add colour to your cards. Watercolour paints are also subtle so use them when you want to achieve a more delicate finish.

2 glitter glue comes in different colours and applicator sizes to control the flow of the glue.

3 felt tip pens available in a huge array of colours and inexpensive to buy.

4 gel pens come in a rainbow of colours to include sparkles and metallic. The ink is opaque and works beautifully on dark-coloured cards.

5 brush markers double-ended felt pens with a narrow point for intricate work and a wider one for covering larger areas.

6 colouring pencils and watercolour pencils choose the best quality you can afford. Colours can be blended together to create other shades.

7 kneadable eraser a good quality eraser is essential if you want to remove pencil lines completely. Kneadable erasers are very versatile as they can be moulded to a point.

8 pencil use an HB pencil for guidelines to cut and a 2B pencil or softer for lines you know you will want to rub out.

9 pencil sharpener safer to use than a craft knife for sharpening pencils.

10 round paintbrush good for general painting. A good quality brush will have a smooth tip for detail work. Synthetic brushes are ideal for card colouring.

11 angle paintbrush good for double-loading paint (putting two colours on a brush at a time), to allow you to colour shade and highlight in one go.

12 decorating chalks available in a large range of colours and designed to give a soft finish. Apply with cotton wool buds or stencil brushes. To avoid smudging, fix with a spray of fixative.

Card-making tools and materials

1 light box used for tracing designs and for dry stencil embossing.

2 embossing stencil metal stencil used in conjunction with a light box and an embossing tool for a technique referred to as dry embossing.

3 cutting mat always choose a self-healing cutting mat, as the surface will close back over the cuts you have made and will remain smooth. Never use the cutting mat when embossing with a heat tool, as this will cause the mat to buckle.

4 guillotine it is now possible to buy small lightweight guillotines that are very useful for cutting paper and card and are easier to use than rolling blade cutters.

5 sticker maker converts small embellishments into stickers by applying an even surface of glue to the reverse of the embellishment.

6 ribbler this hand-held machine simply and quickly corrugates card as it is fed through the rollers. If you like working with corrugated card then invest in one of these as it will soon cover the cost of purchasing finished corrugated card.

7 craft knife a good quality sharp craft knife is a must. An interchangeable blade is far better than a snap-off blade. If your budget allows, invest in a swivel blade for cutting curves.

8 scissors you will need a good pair of decoupage scissors especially when you are cutting out intricate designs. Invest in both a small pair and a larger one for use on larger designs.

9 hammer a small hammer that is not too heavy to hold is ideal for using with an eyelet setter. A pin hammer or tacking hammer are both suitable.

10 eyelet mat designed to provided a clean, hard-wearing surface to create eyelet holes without damaging your cutting mat or work surface.

11 hole punch and setter a combination set designed to punch holes into card stock and set the eyelets.

12 eyelets available in a variety of colors and different shapes and sizes.

13 heat gun manufactured for working with paper. Keep your hands off the vents and hold the gun about 15 cm (6 in) from your project to avoid the paper from scorching.

Stencils and stamping

1 wooden stamps made of a wooden block, a piece of mounting foam and a detail rubber image.

2 metallic stencil cream paints metallic cream colour that is great for stencilling. Apply the cream with a stencil brush or cotton wool bud. Clean the brushes with soap and water after use.

3 stencil brush available in a variety of sizes. Use the appropriate size for the design you are working with.

4 metal stencil template metal templates are extremely durable and mostly used for outlining, cutting or dry stencil embossing.

5 embossing tool used for scoring paper and card and for stencil embossing.

6 decorative punch available in all shapes and designs, decorative punches are used to repeat a design by punching silhouette paper shapes as decoration.

7 sticky stencil a plastic repositionable, self-adhesive stencil. Wash with warm soapy water and replace onto the carrier sheet after use.

8 embossing stencil lightweight brass stencil used for dry stencil embossing.

9 pricking tool long, sharp spike on a wooden or plastic handle. A useful tool for making fine, even holes in paper, vellum or card stock and for lifting off very small stickers.

10 embossing powder sprinkle over wet ink, tap off the excess and heat with a heat gun to melt the powder and give your design a raised finish.

11 pastel embossing powder soft and subtle colour used in the same way as traditional metallic powders. Used to create embossed effects with a heat tool.

12 glitter look out for ultra fine glitter as it is particularly effective for card making.

13 pigment-based ink pad available in clear or tinted, it stays wet for about 10 minutes to allow a longer application time. Used with embossing powder, it creates raised images when rubber stamping.

14 3-D gloss a thick, viscous fluid that is opaque when wet and dries clear. It leaves the surface 'glass-like' and raised. Ideal for use on any porous surface.

15 dye-based ink pad water-based and very fast drying, it can be used not only for stamping but also to create watercolour effects using a paintbrush and water.

16 embossing ink pad available in clear or tinted. The ink is slow drying on the card so stays moist while you apply embossing powders to create raised images when stamping.

STICKERS

Autumn leaves 16

Daisy, daisy 18

Let's get moving 20

3-D butterflies 30

Christmas bauble 33

Bouquet of flowers 36

Pretty parcel 23

Tulip time 26

Bonny bib 28

Perfect pressed flowers 39

Mini card and envelope 42

Wedding celebration 45

Sticker techniques

Stickers are far more than just an outline or design applied to the front of a card. There are numerous designs to choose from and in this chapter you will find ideas and inspiration on how to make the most of their simplicity. Stickers can be cut out, coloured in and positioned back-to-back to create amazing three-dimensional effects. They are easy to use and so provide the perfect starting point for someone who has never made greeting cards before.

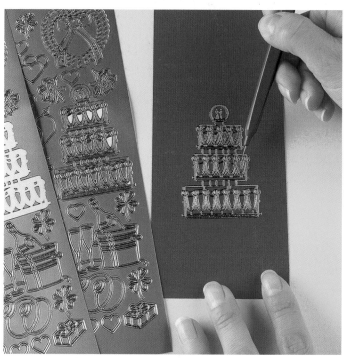

Cutting out to create coloured backgrounds

Remove the outline sticker from the backing sheet and stick it onto a piece of coloured card. Cut around the edges of the sticker. This card-backed sticker can now be used for embellishing a card. Apply 3-D foam glue pads to the back to add further dimension.

Creating two-tone designs

You will need two different coloured outline stickers of the same design. Take the outline of one sticker and stick it onto a piece of white or coloured card or acetate. Use the pricking tool to pick up the small background pieces from the other sticker of the same design to fill in the holes of the main sticker.

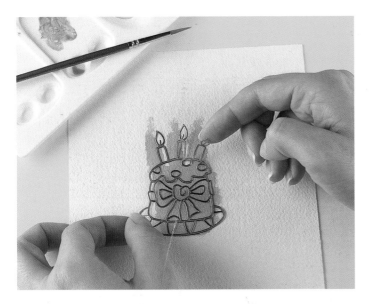

Colouring in outline stickers with paints

Choose an outline sticker and, using watercolour paints, roughly paint the design of the sticker onto a piece of watercolour paper or good quality card stock. The paper will have to be quite thick to avoid it cockling. When the paint is dry, stick the sticker over the design and cut out around the edges, ready to use for your card design.

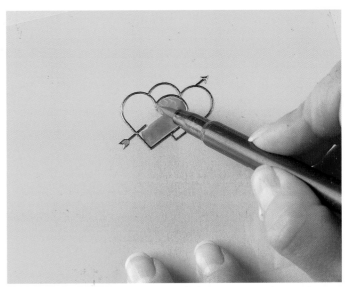

Colouring in outline stickers with permanent markers

To create a stained glass effect, position the outline sticker onto a piece of acetate and use coloured permanent marker pens to fill in the background. When dry, cut out leaving a border around the edges of the sticker to allow the acetate to fit in the aperture of a card.

Using rubdown stickers

Rubdowns are a great way to add an embellishment to a card. Choose the rubdown of your choice, cut it out from the backing sheet and position it onto a piece of card. Using a flat wooden stick, rub over the design applying gentle pressure. Peel off the backing sheet to reveal the rubdown. Layer the card on coloured backgrounds to suit the design of your card.

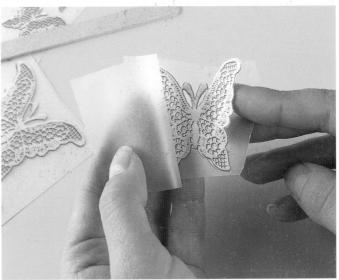

Back-to-back positioning

Stickers can be positioned back to back to create a two-dimensional effect. Great for hanging inside aperture cards. Simply select two stickers of the same design and place them back to back. Sandwich thread or fine cord between the two layers and attach inside a card aperture.

Autumn leaves

Rich reds, browns and greens all combine together to make this card stand out from the rest. The unusual shape of the card makes it look more difficult to make than it actually is.

YOU WILL NEED

A4 burgundy card
Cutting mat
Craft knife
Ruler
Pencil

Compass
Selection of autumn leaves and
  flowers stickers
Talcum powder

1 Transfer the harmonica template on page 122 onto the burgundy card and mark the fold and cut lines. Working on the cutting mat, cut out the template and cut along the solid lines using a sharp craft knife and a ruler. Fold the card along the central fold then fold over the top and bottom folds, making sure not to fold the centre extension.

2 With the card in the correct position, draw a circle 6 cm (2½ in) in diameter using the pencil and the compass in the middle of the centre extension and position the autumn leaves around the outline of the circle.

3 Once the circle is complete, position the top embellishment with half the sticker extending past the card's edge. Turn the card over and dab a little talcum powder on the back of the protruding sticker to absorb the glue.

4 Finish off the card by randomly positioning a few fallen leaves to the left hand side of the card along the bottom edge. ■

Daisy, daisy

Bright, fresh and funky is the message this card sends out. It is perfect for a young person or someone young at heart and is guaranteed to brighten anyone's day. Makes a great 'thinking of you' card.

YOU WILL NEED

A4 yellow card
Guillotine
Ruler
Embossing tool
A4 lime green paper

Pencil
Scissors
Glue stick
3 daisy head bead stickers
    in yellow and orange

1 Cut the A4 yellow card in half lengthways using the guillotine. Score the card down the centre lengthways using the ruler and the embossing tool and fold over.

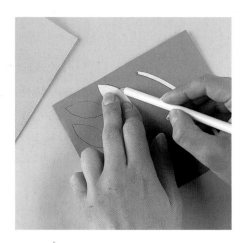

2 Refer to the leaves and stems templates on page 122 and draw the shapes onto the lime green paper then cut them out. Crease the leaves in half to create a three-dimensional effect.

3 Position the green stems and leaves on the front of the card and glue them down. Make sure you glue down only one half of each leaf so that the three-dimensional effect is not lost.

4 Carefully remove the daisy head bead stickers one by one from the backing sheet and position them at the top of the stems to complete the card. ■

Let's get moving

Using outline stickers to make this bright and bold card couldn't be easier. It's perfect for friends or family moving into a new home. Using watercolour paints means the colours can be as bold or as subtle as you like.

YOU WILL NEED

Silver house outline sticker
 8½ x 6½ cm (3½ x 2½ in)
Sheet of acetate
Watercolour paints in blue, green and brown
Water pot

Paintbrush
Paint palette
2 sheets A4 white watercolour card
Ruler
Pencil

Scissors
Sheet of silver border stickers
Glue dots
Embossing tool

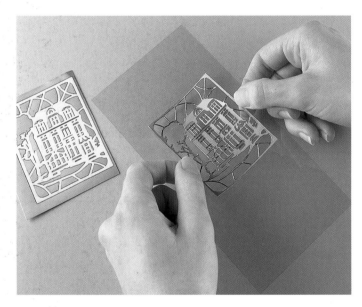

1 Carefully remove the house outline sticker from the backing sheet and position it in the centre of the piece of acetate.

2 Mix a small amount of watercolour paints onto a palette. Use pale blue for the sky, green for the trees and grass, and brown for the house bricks. Using the paintbrush, paint the colours onto one of the A4 white watercolour cards, placing the outline sticker nearby to use as a guide for the position of the colours. **steps 3–6 ▶**

3 Allow the watercolour painting to dry. With a ruler, measure the size of the house outline sticker. Pencil in the measurements onto the watercolour painting or hold the outline sticker over the painting then trim the background so that it fits exactly behind the outline sticker.

4 To frame the house outline sticker, remove one strip at a time from the border sticker sheet and position each strip on the acetate about 1 cm (½ in) from the house sticker. When all four borders are in place, cut around the border.

5 Use glue dots or a small amount of glue on the back of the acetate to attach it to the watercolor background.

6 Score the second A4 white watercolour card down the centre lengthways using ruler and the embossing tool and fold over. Centrally position the design on the front of the card and stick down using a little more glue. ■

Pretty parcel

Everyone should have a little glitter in their life, especially around birthdays and Christmas. This sparkly card is the perfect accompaniment to a gift. You could also accessorize with a matching gift tag to complete the picture.

YOU WILL NEED

Parcel and bow double-sided sticker
   4¹/₂ x 4¹/₂ cm (1¹/₂ x 1¹/₂ in)
Scissors
Small piece of spare white card
Dark blue and silver glitter

A5 silver holographic card
A5 blue sparkle card
A5 duck egg blue pearl card
Pencil
Guillotine

3-D foam squares
A4 white card
Ruler
Embossing tool
Glue stick

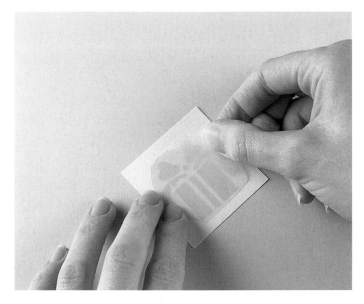

1 Using a pair of scissors, cut out the parcel and bow motif from the rest of the designs on the sheet. Peel off the protective backing sheet and place it sticky side down onto the piece of spare white card. Press down and gently remove the backing sheet to reveal the design which will have a sticky surface.

2 Sprinkle the dark blue glitter over the surface of the design starting at the top and leaving some areas uncovered, then sprinkle the silver glitter towards the bottom of the design. Tap off the excess glitter and return it to the pot. **steps 3–6 ▶**

3 Cut around the parcel, leaving a small border of white card showing.

4 Cut a 7-cm (3-in) square from the silver holographic card, a 6-cm (2½-in) square from the blue sparkle card and a 5-cm (2-in) square from the duck egg blue pearl card, using the pencil to mark the measurements and the guillotine to ensure a straight and even cut.

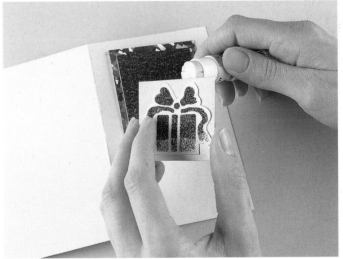

5 Place 3-D foam glue pads onto the back of the parcel, then remove the backing from the foam pads and centrally position the parcel onto the duck egg blue pearl card.

6 Cut the white card to 20 x 15 cm (8 x 6 in) and score it down the centre lengthways using the ruler and the embossing tool then fold over. Glue the silver holographic square onto the front of the white card, followed the blue sparkle square and the duck egg blue pearl square with the parcel. ■

TIP When using scissors for cutting out detail, always hold them at a 90 degree angle from your body and turn the image you are cutting rather than the scissors. This allows you to see the image better, ensuring fewer mistakes and a closer finish.

Tulip time

These tulips look spectacular adorning this pyramid card. Write your greeting message on the inside of the card and send it flat so that your recipient can erect the card him or herself.

1 Photocopy the pyramid template on page 123 and cut it out. Place the template onto the pale lemon card, trace around the outline with a pencil and cut it out carefully using scissors.

2 Using the template as a guide, lightly mark the fold lines and slit for the tab with a pencil. Carefully cut the slit with a craft knife, placing the cutting mat underneath to protect your work surface. Score along the fold lines using the ruler and the embossing tool. Leave a small space at the tip of the pyramid unscored.

3 Place the pyramid card right side up on your work surface and gently remove the large tulip stickers from the backing sheet. Position them as if they are growing from the bottom edge of the card, two per triangle.

4 Finally, remove the smaller tulips from the backing sheet and complete the design by adding five per triangle at the base of the larger tulips. ■

Bonny bib

This unique card will bring a smile to the face of any new mum. Silver peel-offs edge the card for a perfect finish. Pastel cards work equally well for this design.

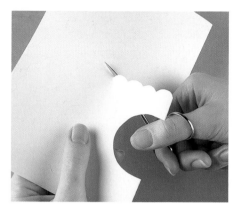

YOU WILL NEED

A4 white card
Ruler
Embossing tool
Pencil
Scissors
Rubber

Silver decorative outline stickers
Silver sticker dots
Pricking tool
Baby girl stickers to include an umbrella, star, teddy bear and duck

1 Using the ruler and the embossing tool, score the A4 white card down the centre lengthways and fold over. Using the bib template on page 124, trace the outline of the shape in pencil onto the folded card, making sure that the design is placed at the edge of the fold. Cut out the design and rub out any pencil marks.

2 To decorate the neck edge of the bib, peel off the decorative outline sticker from the backing sheet and stick it close to the edge, as shown in the picture.

3 The delicate detail around the bib is created using tiny sticker dots. Use the pricking tool to pick up each individual dot and place it in position.

4 Finally, gently remove the pre-made baby sticker from the backing sheet and position it on the front of the card just below the neck edge. ■

3-D butterflies

This three-dimensional holographic card really stands out from the crowd. Combine silver outline stickers with holographic outline stickers and textured card for perfect results.

YOU WILL NEED

Red holographic sticker
 9 x 9 cm (7½ x 7½ in)
Sheet of acetate
Scissors

A5 gold card
Ribbler
Glue dots
White A4 card

Ruler
Embossing tool
3 butterfly outline stickers

1 Carefully remove the red holographic sticker from the backing sheet and position it onto the piece of acetate. Cut the acetate to the size of the sticker.

2 Use the ribbler to create a corrugated effect on the gold card. Hold the tool in one hand and feed the card between the rollers. Turn the handle and watch the ribbled card come out the other end. Cut the ribbled card so that it is slightly larger than the red sticker. **steps 3–6 ▶**

3 Centrally glue down the acetate with the sticker onto the ribbled card using glue dots placed on the back of the sticker.

4 Cut a 22 x 11-cm (9 x 4½-in) rectangle from the white card and score it down the centre lengthways using the ruler and the embossing tool and fold over. Position the ribbled card and sticker on the front of the white card and glue in place.

5 You will need three butterfly stickers to achieve a 3-D butterfly. Remove the first butterfly from the backing sheet and fold it in half, sticky side out. Do the same with the second butterfly and place the sticky side of the left wing of butterfly two on the sticky side of the right wing of butterfly one so that the wings overlap each other. Repeat the same process for butterfly three but stick its right wing to the left wing of butterfly one.

6 Open up the butterfly and, taking care not to allow the two remaining sticky wings to come into contact with each other, place them onto the centre of the holographic sticker and press down to stick into place. ■

Christmas bauble

This is a Christmas card with a difference. The velvet bauble sticker is beautifully displayed when hanging freely in the aperture of the card. Simple and quicker than you would think to make, this card is perfect for sending out to family and friends over the festive period.

YOU WILL NEED

Scissors
A4 white card
Pencil
Cutting mat
Craft knife

Ruler
Embossing tool
2 red flock bauble stickers
Red thread
Left-overs from outline stickers in gold

Pricking tool
Gold border sticker
Glue stick
Hole punch or eyelet maker
Gold ribbon

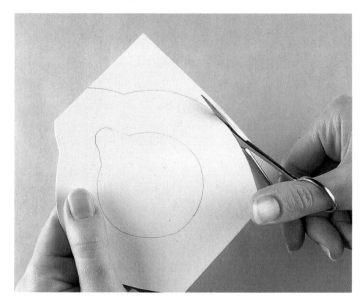

1 Photocopy the bauble template on page 124 and cut it out. Place the template onto the white card and trace around the outline with a pencil. Fold the card in half along Fold 1 and cut out the outline. Open the card and place it flat on the cutting mat. Cut out the aperture with the craft knife. Fold the card over again and trace around the cut aperture so that it is transferred onto the other side of the card. Cut it out, using the craft knife. With the ruler and the embossing tool, score along Folds 2 and 3 and fold over.

2 To make the bauble, remove the first bauble sticker from the backing sheet, and place it onto your work surface sticky side up. Position the red thread onto the bauble making sure there is sufficient thread coming out of the top of the bauble with which to hang it. Remove the second bauble and place it on top of the first bauble so that the sticky sides are together. **steps 3–6 ▶**

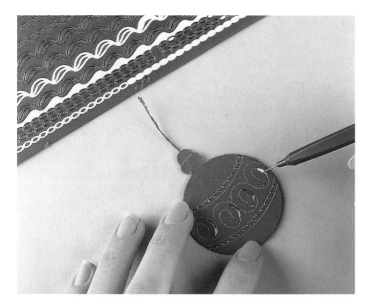

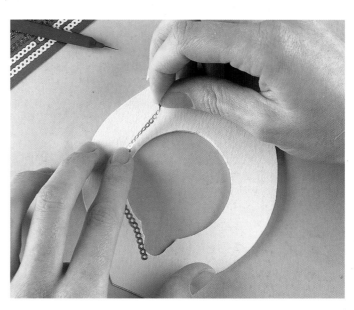

3 Using the small elements that are left over when outline stickers have been used for another design, decorate both sides of the bauble. Use a pricking tool to pick up very small pieces.

4 Remove the gold border sticker from the backing sheet and position it around both the front and back apertures of the card.

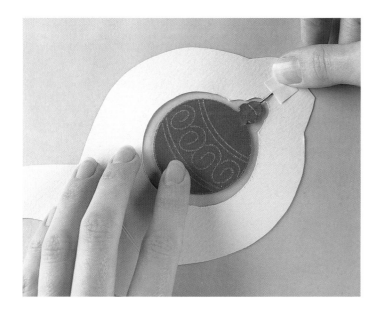

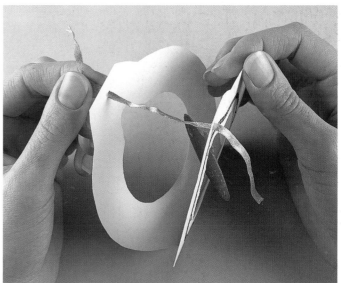

5 Open the card flat, and with the wrong side uppermost, attach the end of the red thread to the card using a small piece of white paper and glue.

6 Fold the card over and make a small hole at the top (one on either side) using a hole punch or an eyelet maker, and thread the gold ribbon through both holes, securing with a pretty bow. ■

Bouquet of flowers

Send this beautiful bouquet of flowers as a perfect get-well-soon card or simply just to say hello. Definitely a card for the cherished recipient to treasure.

YOU WILL NEED

A4 white card
Ruler
Embossing tool
Decorative scissors (Victorian wide)
A5 lemon diamond pattern vellum

Pricking tool
A5 purple striped vellum
Iris and daffodil bouquet rubdown
    11-cm (4½-in) high
Lolly stick

Scissors
Glue dots
Gold ribbon

1 Cut the A4 white card to 20 x 15 cm (8 x 6 in). Score it down the centre lengthways using the ruler and the embossing tool and fold over. Using the decorative edge scissors, align the top edge of the scissors with the front edge of the card and trim the card to leave a fancy finish.

2 Cut the lemon vellum to fit the front of the white card and edge the right hand side with the decorative edge scissors. Using the border made by the decorative scissors as a guide, make a continuous row of small holes using the pricking tool on both the white card and the yellow vellum.
steps 3–6 ▶

3 Cut out the iris and daffodil rubdown from the backing sheet. Remove the backing sheet and position the rubdown onto a piece of purple striped vellum. Rub a lolly stick firmly over the surface of the rubdown to release it from the carrier sheet then gently peel off the carrier sheet.

4 Using small scissors, carefully trim around the floral design to leave a small border of purple.

5 Using glue dots, stick the yellow vellum onto the front of the white card followed by the purple vellum with the floral sticker.

6 Tie a small bow from the gold ribbon and position it over the stems of the flowers, using a glue dot to hold it in place. ■

Perfect pressed flowers

These rub-on copies of pressed flowers look fabulous and are far easier to work with than the real thing. Layers of colour complement the flowers and the eyelets finish off the design beautifully.

YOU WILL NEED

A4 white card	A5 white card	Eyelet mat
Ruler	Lolly stick	Eyelet punch and setter
Embossing tool	A5 red pearl card	Hammer
Scissors	Guillotine	4 brass eyelets
Flower rub-on 8 x 8 cm (3¼ x 3¼ in)	Glue stick	

1 Cut a 25 x 12½-cm (10 x 5-in) rectangle from the A4 white card and score it down the centre using the ruler and the embossing tool. Fold over and set aside. Cut out the flower rub-on from the rest of the sheet and carefully remove the backing sheet.

2 Cut an 9-cm (3½-in) square from the A5 white card. Centrally position the rub-on onto it and rub the lolly stick firmly over the surface of the rub-on to release it from the carrier sheet. Gently peel off the carrier sheet.
steps 3–6 ▶

3 Cut the red pearl card to an 11-cm (4½-in) square using the guillotine and position a 10-cm (4-in) square of white card in the middle of the red card and glue in place. Glue both cards onto the front of the blank greeting card set aside from Step 1, ensuring they are positioned centrally.

4 To make the eyelet holes in each of the four corners, position the card face up on the eyelet mat and place the eyelet punch in one corner, hold the tool at its base, and, keeping it vertical, hit the top of the hole punch hard with the hammer – once should be enough. Repeat on all corners.

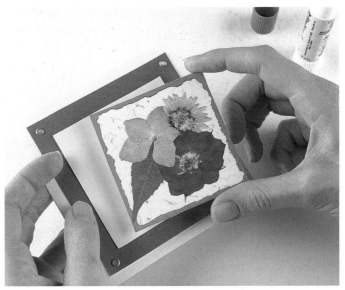

5 Turn the card over. Position the eyelets one at a time, eyelet side down on the mat. Position the holes directly over each eyelet so that the barrel of the eyelet shows through the card. Put the eyelet setter into the eyelet, and, holding it close to the card, hit it sharply with the hammer. The idea is to flatten the back of the eyelet to secure it in place.

6 Assemble the card by placing the mounted rub-on in the centre of the front of the card and glue it in position. ■

TIP When making holes for eyelets, work over an eyelet mat as cutting mats can get damaged.

Mini card and envelope

Try something a little different with this cute envelope card. It's amazing how a simple paper folding technique can look so effective, using hand-made mulberry paper for extra effect. Why not create a matching gift tag and make your gift wrapping something to remember.

YOU WILL NEED

A5 lilac card
Ruler
Embossing tool

Scissors
Sheet of lilac hand-made mulberry paper
Paintbrush

Glue stick
Pre-embossed tulip design, large and small
Sticker maker

1 Turn the A5 lilac card over so the wrong side of the card is uppermost. Using the ruler and the embossing tool, score down the centre lengthways and fold over. Set aside. To make the miniature envelope, cut a 10 x 20-cm (4 x 8-in) rectangle from the lilac mulberry paper and fold it in half lengthways and crease the fold. Now fold the paper in half vertically and crease the second fold. The original piece of paper has now been quartered.

2 Position the folded edge of the hand-made paper closest to your body and unfold the second fold. Fold the top left and right corners into the centre, making sure the two triangles meet. **steps 3–6** ▶

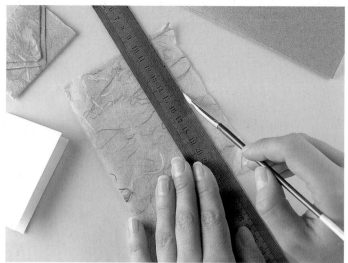

3 Fold the point over so that it touches the bottom folded edge. Fold the two remaining edges into the centre, as in the previous step. Now fold the point over towards the bottom, about 1 cm (½ in) above the first point.

4 Make a mini card from the remaining piece of white card. Cut it to a 7½ x 10-cm (3 x 4-in) rectangle, fold it in half lengthways and set it aside. Prepare the mulberry paper for mounting onto the mini card. Place the ruler on the paper and run a damp paintbrush down the side of the ruler then tear along the line to achieve soft-feathered egdes. The paper should be slightly smaller than the white card.

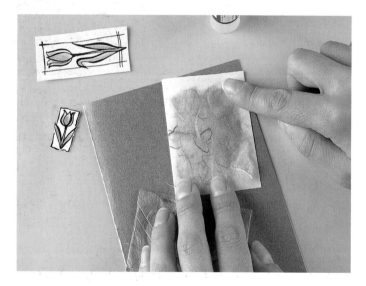

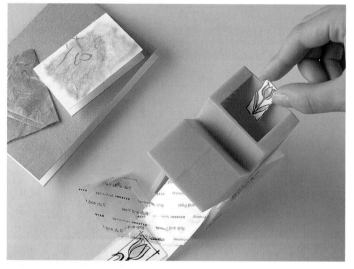

5 Place the mulberry paper on the front of the mini white card and glue it in place. Position the mini envelope and mini card onto the front of the main greeting card at an angle and glue them in place.

6 To make the stickers from the pre-embossed tulip images, pull the adhesive tape until it appears out the bottom of the sticker maker. Drop the images face up into the sticker maker and pull the tape through the machine until the images appear on the tape. Tear the tape and rub gently over the top film before peeling it off to expose the stickers. Remove the stickers from the backing sheet and place them on the front of the mini card and envelope. ■

Wedding celebration

Why not make a card the bride and groom will cherish forever in celebration of their special day. There are so many wedding-themed outline stickers that it is often difficult to choose just the one design. Coupled with the elegant lace effect down the side, this card is a perfect design for a modern or traditional wedding.

YOU WILL NEED

A5 pink card	Cutting mat	A5 sheet of vellum
Ruler	Craft knife	Pink gel pen
Embossing tool	Glue dots	Scissors
Lacé template 13 x 2½ (5 x 2 in)	Silver wedding cake outline sticker	Background cards in silver, pink and white
Low tack masking tape	7 x 4½ cm (3 x 2 in)	Glue stick

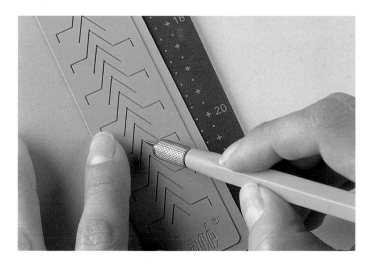

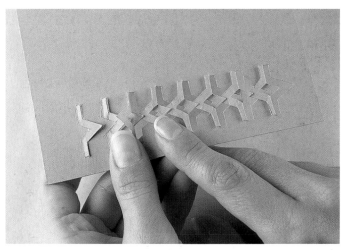

1 Turn the A5 pink card over so that the wrong side is uppermost. Score down the centre of the card using the ruler and the embossing tool and fold over. Place the open card flat on your work surface and position the lacé template on the right hand edge of the front of the card, holding it in place with low tack masking tape. Place a cutting mat beneath the card and, using the lacé template as a guide and a sharp craft knife, cut into the card following the lines of the template, making sure that the craft knife cuts right into the corners of the template lines.

2 Carefully remove the lacé template. Hold the card in your hand, right side up. Working from right to left, release the first cut shape and fold it down. Repeat with each of the cut shapes in turn, tucking the triangular points one beneath the other to hold them in place. Use a glue dot to hold the last one down. **steps 3–6 ▶**

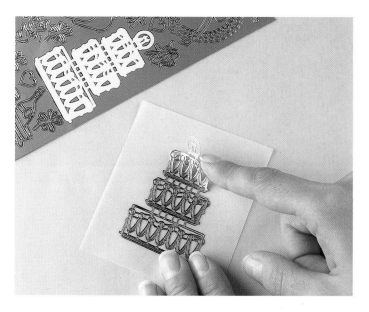

3 Gently remove the wedding cake outline sticker from the backing sheet and position it onto the piece of vellum.

4 Use the pink gel pen to colour in the vellum background behind the outline sticker, taking care to leave some of the vellum background showing through.

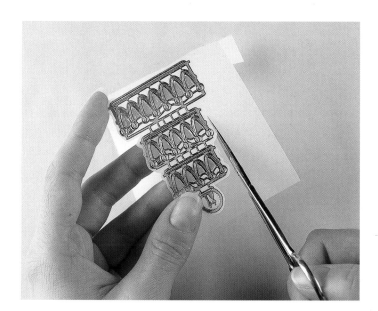

5 With a pair of scissors cut around the wedding cake outline sticker, as close to the edge of the sticker as possible. Hold the scissors still as you close the blades and turn the vellum – this will ensure a smooth edge.

6 Cut the background cards to size so that each layer is slightly bigger than the other, starting with the silver, then pink and finally white. Position the background rectangles centrally on the front of the card and glue each layer down. When working with vellum, stick the background layers down first, layering towards the vellum and sticking the vellum layer last. ■

STENCILS

Sea shells 52

Leafy tag 55

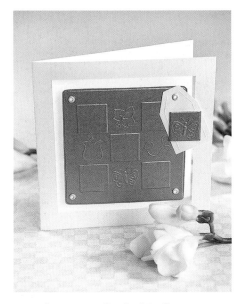

Embossed delight 58

Golden parcels 68

Sail away 70

Flower power 72

Spirelli rose 61

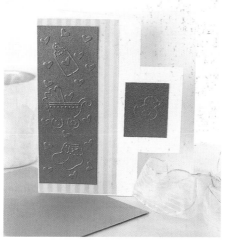

Baby boom 64

Geometric squares 66

Sparkly Christmas tree 75

Perfect poppy 78

Handbags and gladrags 81

Stencil techniques

Stencilling is simple, effective and gives great results. With a multitude of designs and materials readily available, it is possible to achieve a broad range of finishes. Sticky stencils are a new generation of stencils, repositionable and self-adhesive. Because they are made of rubber they are very pliable and are suitable to use on both flat and curved surfaces. They can also be used for dry embossing or regular stencilling. Plastic stencils require a thin film of spray adhesive to create a temporary bond with the surface to be stencilled. Metal stencils are not suitable for regular stencilling because the contact between the stencil and the surface is not usually tight enough to stop colour bleeding under the stencil, however, they are fabulous to use for dry embossing and give a very effective raised finish.

Securing non-metallic stencils in place

To secure the stencil in place and ensure that when colouring in the colour doesn't bleed, it is important to have a tight contact between the stencil and the surface being stencilled. Use spray adhesive to provide a sticky back to the stencil. Place the stencil on a piece of paper and, holding the can approximately 25 cm (10 in) away from the stencil, spray it evenly. Always work in a well-ventilated room when doing this. Place the stencil sticky-side-down on the paper, ready for colouring in.

Colouring stencil designs

There are several ways to colour in stencils. The most popular is to use stencil paint or stencil creams. Dab a small amount of paint onto a stencil brush and use a piece of kitchen paper to remove the excess. Tap the brush lightly onto the stencil and use a clean brush each time you change colour. When you have finished colouring in, peel of the stencil and wash it in warm soapy water. You can also use chalks and watercolour paints but take care as the bond between the stencil and the surface must be tight enough to prevent the paint bleeding under the stencil.

Securing metal stencils in place

Metal stencils such as those used for mola cutting, lacé and silhouette cutting need to be secured to the card with low tack masking tape. Mola cutting differs from silhouette cutting in that a silhouette template is more often a picture rather than a modular design.

Cutting from metal stencils

Place the secured stencil over a cutting mat to protect your work surface. When cutting using a craft knife, it is important that the blade is sharp so change the blade regularly. Place the knife point as close as possible to the sides of the stencil with the handle vertical then lower the handle and draw the blade so that it comes into contact with the card.

Securing embossing stencils in place

The most popular use for metal stencils is dry embossing, a simple technique that requires a light box. Secure the metal stencil in place onto the light box with low tack masking tape before you start work.

Embossing technique

With the stencil taped in place, switch on the light box and position the card over the stencil, wrong side uppermost. Use the embossing tool to make indentations in the card. Use the largest, most rounded size tool that fits your stencil to avoid tearing the card (a smaller tool head will be sharper, therefore increasing the risk of tearing the card). Pressing down firmly, draw the tool against the edges of the stencil. When you have completed the stencil's outline, turn the card over to check that the design shows through clearly.

Sea shells

These magical foil sea shells bring a unique look to your greeting card. Combine them with textured paper to complete the look.

YOU WILL NEED

A5 white card	Scissors	A4 ivory pearl card
3 sticky sea shell stencils	A5 pearl white card	Ruler
Adhesive paste	Ribbler	Embossing tool
Spatula	A5 blue mirror card	Glue stick
A5 sheet of blue metallic foil	A5 aqua blue card	3-D foam glue pads

1 Place the three sticky sea shell stencils onto the A5 white card. Rub over using a finger to ensure a good adhesion to the card surface.

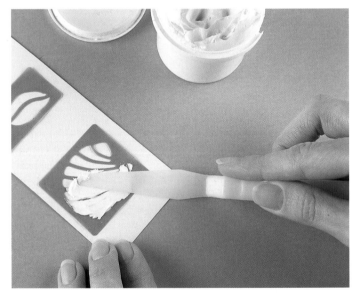

2 Apply the adhesive paste generously over the stencils using the spatula. Take time to work back and forth over the stencils to ensure a smooth finish. As the foil that will be placed over them is so fine, any bumps in the adhesive will show through. Carefully peel away the stencils from the card and wash them in warm soapy water. Leave the adhesive to dry for about 30 minutes. **steps 3–6 ▶**

3 Lay the blue metallic foil metallic side up over the adhesive. Rub over the foil using your finger to ensure the foil has stuck completely.

4 Slowly peel away the foil from the surface of the adhesive. If any pieces of adhesive are not covered with the foil repeat the process. Using the scissors cut around the foiled images, leaving a small border around the edges of each shell.

5 To make the backing layer, feed the pearl white card through the ribbler to create a ribbled effect. Cut the ribbled card to a 7¹/₂-cm (3-in) square. Next, cut the blue mirror card to an 8¹/₂-cm (3¹/₂-in) square. Finally, cut the piece of aqua blue card to a 9¹/₂-cm (4-in) square.

6 Score the A4 ivory pearl card down the centre lengthways using the ruler and the embossing tool. To assemble the card, start building up the layers. Stick the aqua blue card to the front of the ivory pearl card, followed by the blue mirror card and finally the ribbled white card. Place a 3-D foam glue pad on the back of the each shell and position over the ribbled card. ■

Leafy tag

Layered hand-made papers add such an ethnic feel to any greeting card. A little simple stencilling in natural colours combined with cord and brads (fasteners) complete the look for a very unusual card.

YOU WILL NEED

Small piece of white card
Sticky leaf stencil 6 x 4½ cm (2½ x 2 in)
Stencil brush
Stencil paints in green, yellow and brown
Kitchen towel
Scissors

Eyelet mat
Eyelet setter
Hammer
White string
A5 hand-made mulberry papers
    in dark green and lime green

Ruler
Paintbrush
A5 pale green card
Embossing tool
Glue stick
Paper brad

1 Place the sticky leaf stencil on a piece of white card large enough to hold the stencil and rub over using your finger to ensure a good adhesion to the card surface. Colour in the leaf design with the stencil brush, using a mix of green, yellow and brown stencil paints. Wipe off any excess paint from the stencil brush with kitchen towel. Gently pull the stencil away from the card and leave the paint to dry before cutting out the tag. Wash the stencil in warm soapy water.

2 Place the tag on the eyelet mat to protect your work surface. Using the eyelet setter, make a hole in the top two corners of the tag. Hold the eyelet setter vertically and hit the top of it firmly with a hammer. **steps 3–6 ▶**

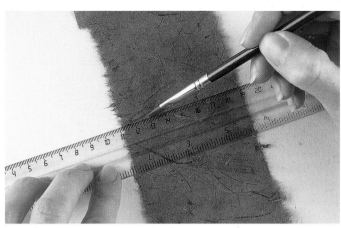

3 Measure a length of white string no more than 7½ cm (3 in) long. Feed the piece of string through each of the holes made by the eyelet setter, tie off on the front of the tag making a small knot in each end of the string.

4 Prepare the mulberry paper for tearing. Place the dark green paper on your work surface and run the wet paintbrush along the edge of the ruler. This softens the paper and makes it easier to tear. Gently tear along the wetted line and repeat for the remaining three sides so that you end up with a rectangle 8 x 12 cm (3 x 5 in) in size. Repeat the process on the lime green paper so that you have a rectangle 6½ x 8 cm (2½ x 3 in) in size.

5 Score the A5 pale green card down the centre lengthways using the ruler and the embossing tool and fold over. Stick the layers of mulberry paper onto the front of the pale green card, mounting the dark green first followed by the lime green.

6 To make the hole for the brad, unfold the card and place the front of it on the eyelet mat. Using the eyelet setter, make a hole in the centre of the front of the card, making sure the hole is central and goes through both layers of handmade paper. Push the paper brad through the hole and pull out the legs to secure the brad. Ensure there is sufficient space to allow the string to hang. Hang the tag with the cord over the brad to complete the card. A gift tag on a present completed in the same way would really complement this card. ■

Embossed delight

This card is brought to life by using a light box and embossing tool to create a dry embossed effect. Embossing is simple and effective. To add further dimension, the card is mounted onto acetate and secured in place with eyelets. The cute butterfly tag adds the finishing touch.

YOU WILL NEED

A5 lilac pearl card
Embossing stencil to include leaf, flower,
    bird, butterfly and square
Light box
Low tack masking tape
Embossing tool
Scissors

Small piece of white card
Glue stick
Sheet of acetate
Eyelet mat
Eyelet setter
Hammer
4 pink eyelets

Ruler
A4 white card
Pencil
Cutting mat
Craft knife

1 Cut the lilac pearl card so that it is slightly larger than the butterfly embossing stencil. Position the stencil onto the light box and secure in place with low tack masking tape. Place the lilac pearl card pearl-side down over the light box and, using the embossing tool, trace around the squares and around the stencil border to create a frame.

2 Emboss the butterfly motif again on a left-over piece of lilac pearl card, using the same technique as before and ensuring the coloured side is face down. Emboss a frame around the outside of the butterfly then cut out. Transfer the tag template on page 125 onto a piece of white card and cut it out. Use the embossing tool to emboss around the border to highlight the design. Glue the lilac butterfly onto the front of the tag, as shown in the final picture. **steps 3–6** ▶

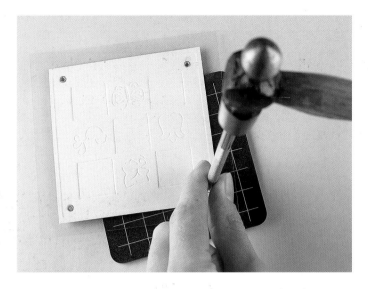

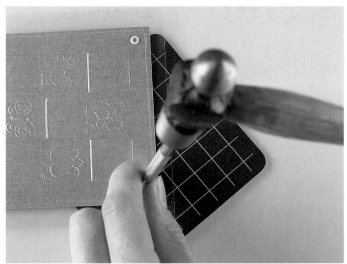

3 Cut the acetate so that it is about 2½ cm (1 in) larger than the lilac pearl card. To secure the lilac card and acetate together, place the acetate centrally onto the back of the card and make a hole in each corner with the eyelet setter and hammer, making sure to place the eyelet mat underneath to protect your work surface.

4 Turn the card over so that the right side is facing you and hammer in three pink eyelets, leaving out the top right eyelet for now. Now place the tag at the top right hand corner of the card and secure into place from the front with the remaining pink eyelet.

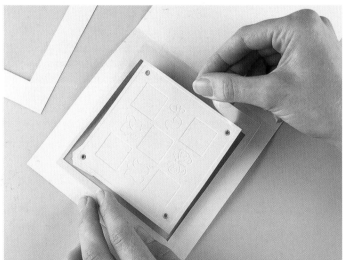

5 Cut the A4 white card to 15 x 28 cm (6 x 11 in). Score the card down the centre lengthways using the ruler and the embossing tool and fold over. To make the aperture, measure the lilac pearl card and pencil in the measurements onto the front of the card. Add another 2½ cm (1 in) to the size of the aperture. Cut around the lines using a craft knife, ensuring you place the opened card on the cutting mat.

6 Finally, assemble the card by sticking the acetate onto the back of the front aperture. ■

Spirelli rose

This card combines the beauty of spirelli with the simplicity of stencilling. Spirelli is the term given to the art of winding decorative threads around card shapes to create kaleidoscope patterns. The shapes can be cut by hand, punched out or bought pre-cut.

YOU WILL NEED

Small piece of white card
Sticky flower stencil 4 x 6 cm (2¹/₂ x 5¹/₂ in)
Stencil paints in red, burgundy and green
2 stencil brushes
Water pot

Scissors
A4 lilac card
Rose metallic thread
Sticky tape
A4 white card

Ruler
Embossing tool
A5 lilac pearl card
Pencil
Glue stick

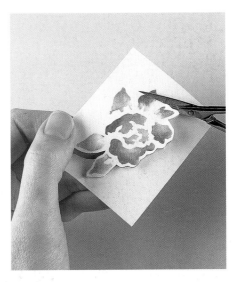

1 Place the sticky flower stencil on a piece of white card large enough to hold the stencil. Mix the red and burgundy stencil paints together to create a rich red, adding a small amount of water to the mix. Colour in the rose petal using the stencil brush.

2 Using a clean stencil brush, mix a small amount of green paint with a little water. Dab this lightly over the leaves to create a watercolour effect.

3 Once the paint has dried, cut around the flower leaving a small border around the design.
steps 4–7 ▶

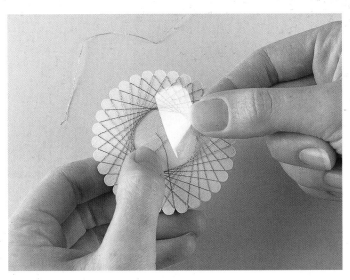

4 Transfer the spirelli template on page 125 onto the piece of lilac card and stick the rose metallic thread to the back of it with a small piece of sticky tape. Turn the shape over and start to wind the thread back and forth, leaving a space of 10 notches between each wind.

5 The pattern will begin to develop quickly as you work. Continue working round, so that each notch has been threaded twice. Once complete, secure the end of the thread at the back with a piece of sticky tape.

6 Score the A4 white card down the centre lengthways using the ruler and the embossing tool and fold over. Reproduce the octagonal template on page 125 onto this card, making sure you place one of the sides along the fold of the card. Cut out the octagonal shape.

7 Using the template on page 125, trace and cut out the shape on the lilac pearl card, face down. Position the lilac shape on the front of the white octagonal card and glue it in place. Position the spirelli shape over the centre of the lilac shape and glue in place. To finish the card, glue the stencilled flower on the front of the spirelli shape. ■

Baby boom

Bonny in blue or pretty in pink, the choice is yours. A lovely card to give to a new mother, guaranteed to take pride of place and to be cherished for years to come. Follow the instructions for a simple introduction to harmonica folding.

A4 white card
Ruler
Embossing tool
Harmonica fold template
Craft knife

Baby embossing stencil to include pram,
    bottle, heart, duck and booties
Light box
Low tack masking tape
A4 pearl blue card

Scissors
Striped blue vellum
Glue stick

1 Cut the A4 white card to 15 x 30 cm (6 x 12 in). Mark the card along the longest edge at 9 cm (3½ in) and then at 18 cm (7 in) and, using the ruler and the embossing tool, score vertically along these marks. Fold the card to the back along the first line and to the front along the second line. Open the card flat and line the central square of the harmonica fold template vertically along the first fold. Cut the three sides of the central square with a craft knife. When the card is folded closed, this square will stand out.

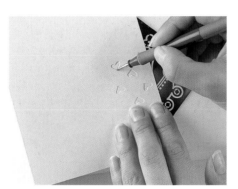

2 Place the heart embossing template onto the light box and secure it in place with low tack masking tape. Place the back of the white card face down over the heart embossing template and, using the embossing tool, randomly emboss the hearts down the outer edge.

3 Cut a 13½ x 5-cm (5½ x 2-in) rectangle from the A4 pearl blue card. Emboss the pram in the centre of the card then the bottle at an angle at the top, the booties at the bottom and randomly placed hearts. Cut another rectangle from the pearl blue card 3½ x 4½ cm (1½ x 2 in) in size. Place it onto the duck stencil face down and emboss using the embossing tool.

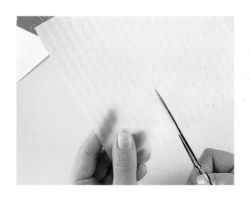

4 Cut out a 15 x 6-cm (6 x 2½-in) rectangle from the striped blue vellum. Glue it to the front left of the card, as shown in the picture.

5 Position the embossed long blue strip over the vellum and stick it in place with glue. Finally, glue down the embossed duck on the right hand side of the card. ■

Geometric squares

Lacé in French means linked together. This refers to the cutting and folding under of the paper flaps on a lacé card. Using duo card makes the effect even more striking. Lacé is detailed and intricate, however, with the proper instructions is very easy to achieve.

YOU WILL NEED

A4 duo red and green card
Pencil
Ruler
Cutting mat
Craft knife

Lacé template 15 x 4 cm (6 x 1³/₄ in)
Low tack masking tape
Lacé craft knife
Glue dots
Gold peel off strips

A4 cream card
Embossing tool
Glue stick

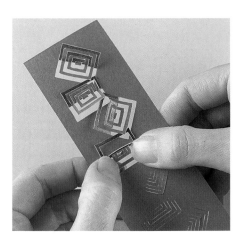

1 Cut a 15 x 5-cm (6 x 2-in) rectangle from the duo red and green card. Mark a border ¹/₂ cm (¹/₂ in) inside the rectangle and cut it out over the cutting mat using the craft knife. Keep the frame aside as you will need it for Step 4.

2 Place the lacé template over the two-tone card, red side up. Secure in place onto the cutting mat using low tack masking tape. Follow the template cutting the design out with the lacé craft knife. Take care when cutting out as the design is quite intricate. Start each cut with the point of the blade pushed into the card and the knife handle vertical, then lower the angle to 45 degrees and draw the knife through the guidelines.

3 Turn the card over and fold back the cut lines. Fold back every other cut line creating a two-toned effect of red and green. If the lines don't stay stuck down just by folding back, use glue dots to secure them in place.

4 Take the cut-out frame from Step 1 and turn it over so that the green side is uppermost. Stick the gold peel off strips centrally around all four sides of the frame, ensuring that the corners are joined and the ends are finished neatly.

5 Cut the A4 cream card to 20 x 20 cm (8 x 8 in). Score the card down the centre lengthways using the ruler and the embossing tool and fold over. Apply some glue to the back of the red lacé strip and stick it down on the front of the card. Finally, stick down the frame which should fit perfectly around the card. The cream background will show through the folded over lacé strips. ■

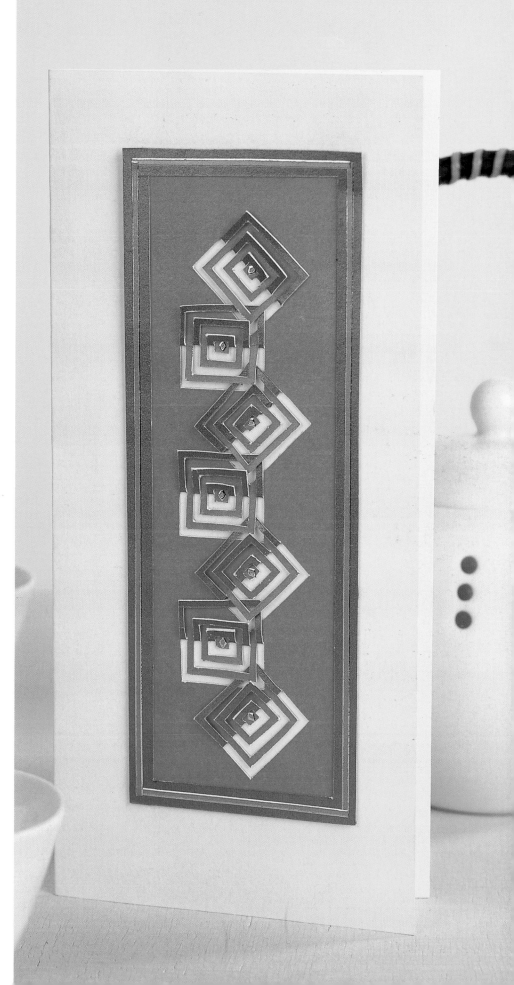

Golden parcels

Keep colours to a simple gold and white for a clean, minimalist look. The parcels have been stencilled for speed and the whole card layered. If you need to make a birthday card in a hurry, this is the perfect solution.

1 Place the sticky parcel stencil on a piece of white card large enough to hold the stencil and rub over it with your finger to ensure a bond between the stencil and the card. Use a cotton bud to shade in the stencil with the gold stencil cream. Carefully peel off the stencil from the card and make two more parcels in the same way.

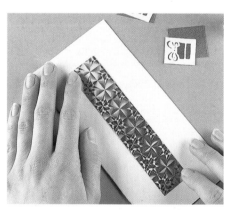

2 Once the parcels are dry, cut them out leaving a small frame around the edges. Cut out a 20-cm (8-in) square from the A4 white card. Score the card down the centre using the ruler and the embossing tool and fold over.

3 Cut out three squares slightly larger than the size of the cut-out parcel squares from the gold card. On the gold holographic card, measure a rectangle 3 x 16 cm (1½ x 6½ in) in size and cut it out. Stick it centrally onto the front of the white card.

4 To assemble the card, stick the parcels onto the gold squares. Place a 3-D foam glue pad on each corner of the back of the gold parcels and mount them at an equal distance apart onto the gold holographic strip. ∎

Sail away

This is the perfect card for a man! Shadow silhouette cutting, using a metal stencil template, conjures up images of lazy days on the sea as with this simple yet effective sailboat card.

YOU WILL NEED

A5 white card
Ruler
Embossing tool
Cutting mat
Sailing boat stencil 13 x 6 cm (5 x 5½ in)
Low tack masking tape

Pencil
Craft knife
Stencil brushes
Decorating chalks in blue, green, yellow and red
Fixative

1 Score the A5 white card down the centre lengthways using the ruler and the embossing tool and fold over. Make sure you work over the cutting mat to protect your work surface when making this card. Position the sailing boat stencil onto the front of the card, securing it in place with low tack masking tape.

2 There are two ways to cut out this design. If you are a beginner, trace the outline of the design using a sharp pencil. Make sure you trace as close to the stencil as possible, then remove the tape and stencil from the card and cut along the lines using the craft knife.

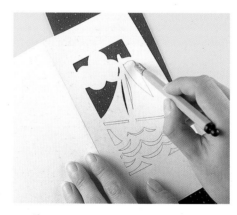

3 If you are more experienced, you can cut out the design against the stencil directly, making sure you keep the craft knife blade as close to the edge of the stencil as possible.

4 Once the stencil has been cut out, open up the card and place it flat on your work surface lined with a sheet of scrap paper. Colour in the waves, the hull, the sails and the clouds using stencil brushes and decorating chalks. Use a clean brush each time you change colour. Finally, fix the colours in place with a light spray of fixative. ■

Flower power

Mola cutting has traditionally been used in textiles. Layers of different fabrics are laid on top of each other, then lines are stitched through to create patterns. The layers are then cut into and peeled away to produce beautiful patchwork. This technique has been adapted for card making with amazing results.

YOU WILL NEED

2 sheets A4 white card	Mola template 10 x 10 cm (4 x 4 in)	A4 sheet of red paper
Scissors	Low tack masking tape	Sheet of silver border stickers
Ruler	Cutting mat	Glue stick
Embossing tool	Craft knife	A5 blue holographic card

1 Cut out a 13-cm (5-in) square from one of the A4 sheets of white card. From the other sheet, cut a rectangle measuring 13 x 26 cm (5 x 10 in). Score the card down the centre lengthways using the ruler and the embossing tool and fold over.

2 Unfold the card and place the mola template on the front of it, securing it with low tack masking tape. Place the card on the cutting mat and cut around the shapes using a craft knife. Repeat on the square piece of white card.
steps 3–6 ▶

3 Use a pair of scissors or a guillotine to cut red paper strips 1-cm ($\frac{1}{2}$-in wide) and trim them with the silver border stickers. Make sure you cut enough to go all the way round the frames of the two mola embellishments.

4 Glue the red strips in place onto the two mola embellishments, cutting the corners at a 45-degree angle for a really professional finish.

5 Cut the blue holographic card so that it is slightly larger than the mola template. Position the front of the card featuring the mola embellishment onto the blue holographic card and glue in place from the back.

6 Diagonally position the second mola embellishment onto the front of the card and secure in place with glue. Trim the corners so that they are flush with the sides of the card. ■

Sparkly Christmas tree

If you can't have glitter at Christmas then when can you have it? Try this perfect last-minute card idea. Quick and easy stencilling achieves instant results.

YOU WILL NEED

Spare piece of white card
Sticky Christmas tree stencil
   5 x 4 cm (2 x 1½ in)
Green pigment-based ink pad
Silver glitter

Scissors
A5 green metallic card
A5 green velvet card
Glue stick
A5 white card

Ruler
Embossing tool
Red glitter glue

1 Place the Christmas tree stencil on a piece of white card large enough to hold the stencil. Rub over it with your finger to ensure a good adhesion to the card surface.

2 Stamp the green ink pad onto the stencil. It is important to use a pigment-based pad as the ink needs to remain wet while you sprinkle glitter onto it. Make sure the stencil is completely covered with the ink. **steps 3–6** ▶

3 Carefully peel off the stencil and wash it in warm soapy water. While the ink is still wet, sprinkle it generously with the silver glitter. Tap off the excess glitter and return it to the pot. Set aside to dry.

4 When the Christmas tree design is dry, cut it out around the border using a pair of scissors. Round off the corners for a softer, less formal finish.

5 Cut the green metallic card so that it is 2½ cm (1 in) larger than the Christmas tree medallion. Next, cut out the green velvet card so that it is 1 cm (½ in) larger than the green metallic card. Stick the medallion onto the metallic card then stick the metallic card onto the velvet card.

6 Score the A5 white card down the centre lengthways using the ruler and the embossing tool and fold over. Stick the matted three layers on the front of the card. Finish off the design by squeezing a small amount of red glitter glue on top of the tree. ■

Perfect poppy

Try your hand at shading through a stencil to create this bright and fresh card. You can achieve a fabulous result using acrylic paints. There are many other methods of colouring in stencils, all of which are described on page 50.

...described on page 50.

YOU WILL NEED

Plastic poppy stencil 10 x 4 cm (4 x 1½ in)
Repositionable poppy stencil adhesive
Spare piece of white card
Stencil paints in red, yellow and green
Stencil brush
Kitchen paper

Scissors
Pencil
Ruler
A5 orange card
Ribbler
A5 yellow card

A4 white card
Embossing tool
Glue stick
3-D foam glue pads

1 To ensure the paint does not bleed beneath the stencil, spray it with repositionable stencil adhesive before positioning it, adhesive side down, onto a piece of white card large enough to hold the stencil. Make sure you work in a well-ventilated room. If the stencil is one of the new generation of sticky stencils, you can work without the spray adhesive and place the stencil straight onto the card, rubbing over it with your finger to ensure a good adhesion to the card surface.

2 Mix a small amount of red and yellow stencil paint together and dab it onto the poppy petals with the stencil brush. Wipe off the excess paint onto a piece of kitchen paper before applying the paint to the stencil.
steps 3–6 ▶

3 To colour in the leaves, start with a little green on the stencil brush, but pick up a small amount of yellow, to brighten the green. This will ensure that the leaves look really fresh. To complete the flower head, fill in the centre with a small amount of dark green paint. Set aside to dry and wash your stencil brushes in warm soapy water.

4 Cut out the poppy picture leaving a frame around the poppy. You may want to pencil in the frame first to ensure a straight, even cut.

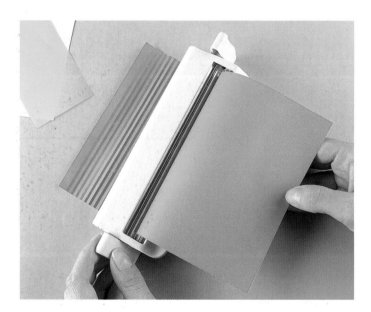

5 Feed the orange card through the ribbler. Turn the handle and watch the corrugated card come out the other end then cut the card so that it is slightly larger than the white poppy card. Cut out a rectangle of yellow card slightly larger than the ribbled card so that it will show when placed beneath the orange rectangle.

6 Cut the A4 white card to a 20-cm (8-in) square. Score it down the centre using the ruler and the embossing tool and fold over. To assemble the card, glue the yellow card onto the front of the white card. Apply 3-D foam glue pads to the ribbled card and poppy picture and stick each layer down in place starting with the yellow card, followed by the ribbled card and finally the poppy picture.

Handbags and gladrags

Every girl needs a handbag! Try this great card idea which is perfect for an 18th or 21st birthday celebration. Vary the colour scheme to suit your recipient's preferences.

YOU WILL NEED

A4 white card	Craft knife	Embossing tool
Pencil	Cutting mat	Light box
Scissors	Metal ruler	15 cm (6 in) orange gingham ribbon
A4 pale lemon card	Embossing stencil to include	Glue dots
Eraser	flower and bow designs	

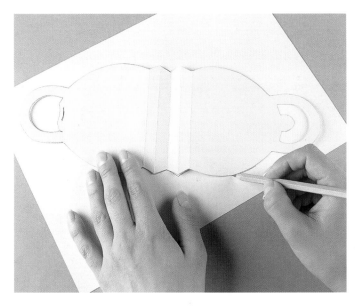

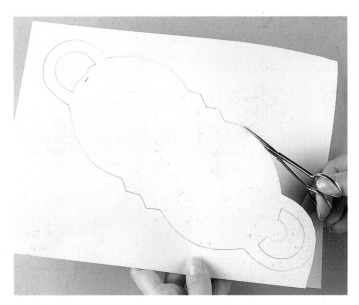

1 Transfer the handbag template on page 125 onto the A4 white card and cut it out. This template can be used again should you want to make this card for another occasion so make sure you save it. Using the template you have cut out from the white card, trace the outline carefully onto the reverse side of the pale lemon card.

2 Cut out the handbag shape and erase any pencil marks. Cut the slit and the tab using the craft knife, ensuring you place the card on the cutting mat first to protect your work surface. **steps 3–6 ▶**

3 On the reverse side of the card, score the base of the handbag along all five fold lines using the metal ruler and the embossing tool to create the folds that will help the card stand up.

4 Place the flower and bow embossing stencil over the light box and position the handbag card with the lemon side facing down over the stencil. Use the embossing tool to trace the flower design across the front and back of the card. After you have embossed a few flowers lift the card to check how the design is taking shape. Emboss the bow just below the handle using the same method.

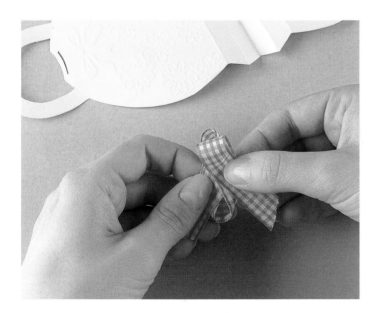

5 To make the knot, take the gingham ribbon and make each end into a loop. Hold one loop in each hand and cross over the two loops. Fold the front loop over the back loop and pass it through the hole in the middle, back to the front. Pull both loops to tighten the bow. Adjust the symmetry of the bow by pulling the tails until they are even.

6 To finish off the card, attach the bow to the front of the card with a glue dot placed underneath the knot. Slot the tab in the slit and fold it over to close the card. You can write your message on the inside of the card. ■

STAMPS

Gentleman's relish 88

Golden daisies 91

Let it snow 94

Musical notes 104

Frosty winter tree 107

Balloons galore 110

Delightful daisy tags 96

Beautiful butterflies 99

Enamelled flower 102

Enamelled heart 113

Sunflowers and butterflies 116

A dalliance with dragonflies 119

Stamping techniques

Rubber-stamping is the stepping stone for many different design elements. Accomplish rubber-stamping and the card-making world is your oyster. When rubber stamping, it is important to work with the correct ink. Use a dye-based ink pad for basic rubber stamping and a pigment-based ink pad for embossing.

BASIC RUBBER STAMPING

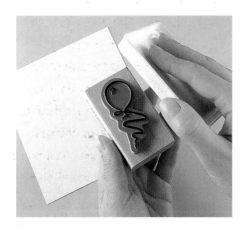

Inking the stamp

Lightly tap the dye-based ink pad onto the face of the rubber stamp so that it is evenly coated with ink. Don't rub the pad against the stamp as the ink may smudge the design.

Stamping the image

Work on a flat, stable surface and place the stamp face down onto your chosen support. Press down along the whole surface of the stamp with your fingers to transfer the ink to the paper or card, ensuring you do not rock the stamp as this may cause the image to blur. Lift the stamp off cleanly to reveal the image.

EMBOSSING

Embossing a stamped image

Work with a pigment-based ink pad as the ink will stay wet long enough to sprinkle with embossing powder. Lightly tap the stamp with the pad so that it is evenly coated with ink. Make sure the ink does not get onto the edges of the stamp. Stamp the image onto your chosen support.

Applying the embossing powder

Work over a piece of scrap paper and sprinkle the wet ink with embossing powder. Tap off the excess onto the scrap of paper and return the powder to the pot. You will have to work quite quickly so that the ink does not dry before applying the powder to it.

DOUBLE EMBOSSING

Inking the paper
When using more than one layer of embossing powder (a technique called double embossing), take a pigment-based ink pad and press it onto a piece of card, using the entire surface area of the ink pad.

Covering with embossing powder
While the ink is still wet, sprinkle the inked paper with embossing powder and tap off the excess, returning it to the pot. Heat the powder with a heat gun and while the powder is still hot and slightly molten, sprinkle a second layer of embossing powder and heat again. The powder will melt and change colour more quickly the second time.

Brushing off excess powder
Every little speck of embossing powder will show when the image is heated. Use a small, clean, dry paint brush to brush off any unwanted powder that remains after tapping off.

Using the heat gun
Heat the embossed image with the heat gun, holding the gun about 15 cm (6 in) away from the image and make sure you keep the gun moving so that the paper does not scorch.

Stamping the image
Whilst the powder is molten and hot, press the stamp onto the wet embossing powder. Hold the stamp still for a few seconds and remove. Take care at this stage as the hot powder can burn.

Cutting out the image
Leave the embossing powder to dry for 10 minutes before cutting out the image. Do not leave it to dry for too long, however, as the embossing powder can harden and crack.

Gentleman's relish

Making interesting cards for male friends or relatives isn't always easy. This shirt design card is ideal for any celebratory occasion such as birthdays, retirement or even a new job. To ensure a perfect looking card, simply co-ordinate the background colours and shirt colours to match.

YOU WILL NEED

A4 bright blue paper
Scissors
Glue stick
A4 pale blue paper

Black dye-based ink pad
Tie rubber stamp 5 cm (2 in)
Spare piece of white card
A4 white card

Ruler
Embossing tool

1 Start by making the shirt. Cut a 21 x 10-cm (8 x 4-in) rectangle from the bright blue paper. Fold the paper in half lengthways and crease the fold. Open up the piece of paper ready for Step 2.

2 Place the piece of paper flat on your work surface. Fold the bottom of the paper 6½ cm (2½ in) up and crease the fold. Unfold the paper again.

3 Fold both the long sides so that each edge touches the centre fold line created in Step 1. Working from the fold line created in Step 2, fold out the right corner diagonally to make a wing. Repeat with the left corner. The diagonal lines should measure approximately 6½ cm (2½ in).
steps 4–8 ▶

4 With the wings at the bottom and facing you, fold the wings up 6½ cm (2½ in) so that they are in the middle of the shirt. Crease the bottom fold.

5 To make the collar fold, cut along the shoulder line from each side 1½ cm (½ in) into the middle. Take the top outside corners of the collar and fold them diagonally to meet in the centre.

6 To make the sleeves, cut ½ cm (¼ in) of the way up the sleeves following the line of the sides of the shirt. Now cut a small triangle out from that point down to the sleeve opening. To finish the shirt, scoop out the back neck of the shirt collar with a pair of scissors. Glue the shirt collar down.

7 To make the tie, stamp the tie rubber stamp once onto a piece of white card large enough to hold the tie stamp and cut it out carefully with scissors. Cut the pale blue paper in half lengthways so that it is A5 size. Lightly tap the black ink pad onto the tie rubber stamp. Stamp the image diagonally across the pale blue paper, making sure your re-ink the stamp as necessary. Trim 1½ cm (½ in) off both one long side and one short side so that this piece of paper is slightly smaller than the front of the white greeting card.

8 Score the A4 white card down the centre lengthways with the ruler and the embossing tool and fold over. To assemble the card, centrally stick the stamped pale blue card onto the front of the white card. Next assemble the shirt onto the remaining piece of pale blue card and cut the card to leave a border around the shirt. Finally, stick the bright blue paper beneath the pale blue paper and place the layers onto the stamped pale blue card and stick into place. ■

Golden daisies

These delightful daisies look lovely in yellow. But by changing the colour of the backing card and the daisies' colour scheme, this card has all the essential elements for any occasion. Quick and easy to make when you need a card in a hurry.

1 Lightly tap the ink pad against the daisy stamp and stamp the design onto a piece of white card large enough to hold the daisy stamp design. Be careful not to rock the stamp as you press down firmly. Lift the stamp cleanly away from the paper and cut out the stamped image, leaving a small white border around the design. Sprinkle the silver embossing powder over the stamped image. Tap off the excess powder and return it to the pot. Now hold the heat gun 15 cm (6 in) away from the stamped image and heat the powder until it melts.

2 Take the A4 white card and, using the ruler and pencil, mark out a 20-cm (8-in) square. Place a cutting mat beneath the card and with the ruler and the craft knife cut along the lines. Score down the centre of the card using the ruler and the embossing tool and fold over. Colour in the daisies using a yellow felt pen. Gentle pen strokes look natural. **steps 3–6 ▶**

3 Cut a piece of gold holographic card about 1¹/₂ cm (¹/₂ in) larger than the daisy design.

4 To add further dimension to the project, apply 3-D foam glue pads to the back of the stamped daisy image.

5 Position the stamped daisy image over the gold holographic card. The 3-D foam pads will act as glue to hold the image in place. Make sure that everything is level and lined up before sticking down the daisies.

6 Position the holographic gold card with the daisy design horizontally onto the front of the white folded card and glue it in place. ■

Let it snow

This cute snow people stamp has been embellished using glitter. Why not make this your Christmas card and send it to your family and friends. Try different colours for the snow people's hats and scarves and choose different backing layers to create an individual look for each card.

YOU WILL NEED

A4 cerise pink card
Ruler
Pencil
Cutting mat
Craft knife
Embossing tool
Deckle-edge scissors

Black dye-based ink pad
Snow people stamp 4 x 9 cm
  (1½ x 3½ in)
Piece of white card
Gel pens in purple, blue, green,
  pink and yellow
Scissors

PVA glue
Holographic glitter
A5 mat gold card
Glue stick

1 Using the ruler and pencil measure a rectangle 15 x 30 cm (6 x 12 in) onto the reverse of the A4 pink card. Cut out the card on a cutting mat using the ruler and the craft knife. Score the card down the centre lengthways using the ruler and the embossing tool and fold over. Use the deckle-edge scissors to give a decorative finish to the edges.

2 Lightly tap the black ink pad onto the snow people stamp then stamp the image onto a piece of white card large enough to hold the image. When positioning the stamp onto the white card, make sure that a large enough border of white shows around the edges of the card. Colour in the design using the gel pens. Cut out the stamped card, leaving a border around the design.

3 Apply PVA glue to the foreground. While the glue is still wet, sprinkle the holographic glitter over the glue, tap away the excess and return it to the pot. Allow the glue to dry for a few minutes before beginning the next stage. Check the bottle for drying times, as they tend to vary between manufacturers.

4 Cut the gold card so that it is about 1½ cm (½ in) taller and 1½ cm (½ in) less wide than the stamped card. Assemble the components of the design horizontally onto the front of the card. Stick down the gold card first followed by the white stamped card, as above. ◼

Delightful daisy tags

Fresh and fun, this daisy stamp is so pretty you simply have to try it out. I have combined tag art with magic mesh to transform the simple lines of the stamp. Give the card to someone who needs a little sunshine in his or her life.

YOU WILL NEED

Double daisy stamp 3 x 8 cm (1¼ x 3¼ in)
Black pigment-based ink pad
A4 white card
Black embossing powder
Heat gun
Felt tip pens in yellow, green and orange

Scissors
2 sheets of A4 pale lemon card
Glue stick
Gold sticky tape 2½-cm (1-in) wide
Self-adhesive yellow magic mesh
Hole punch

White string
A4 bright yellow paper
Ruler
Embossing tool
Pencil

1 Lightly tap the black ink pad onto the double daisy stamp. Stamp the design twice on the A4 white card, re-inking the stamp in the process. Sprinkle the black embossing powder over both of the stamped images. Tap off the excess powder and return it to the pot. Hold the heat gun about 15 cm (6 in) away from the card and heat the embossing powder until it melts, moving the gun continuously so as to not scorch the card. Set aside to dry.

2 Once dry, colour in both of the stamped designs using the yellow felt tip pen for the petals. Use the green felt tip pen for the daisy centres and the leaves. Use orange to colour in the smaller flowers. You can use alternative colours to create an entirely different effect. Carefully cut out both designs. **steps 3–7 ▶**

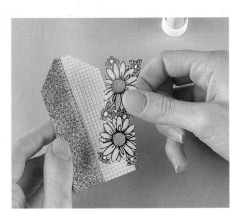

3 Cut a 9 x 3½-cm (3½ x 1½-in) rectangle from one of the pale lemon cards. Cut a 9½ x 4-cm (3¾ x 1½-in) rectangle from the white card. Glue the lemon yellow rectangle onto the white one then centrally glue one of the daisy images from Step 2 over it.

4 Photocopy the tag template on page 126, transfer it onto a piece of white card and cut it out. Then cut a length of gold sticky tape and position it to one side of the tag, trimming off the excess.

5 Cut a piece of the self-adhesive yellow magic mesh to fit the tag. Allow the mesh to slightly overlap onto the gold tape. Trim any magic mesh excess and glue the second daisy image in place.

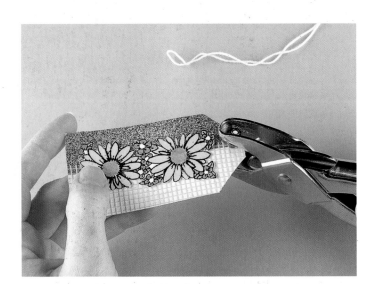

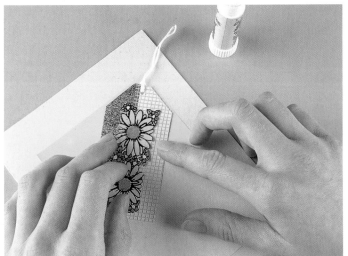

6 Using the hole punch, punch a small hole at the top end of the gift tag. Fold the white string in half and thread it through the hole from the back. Take the loose ends and thread these through the loop, pull tight but make sure not to tear the card.

7 Score the remaining A4 pale lemon card down the centre lengthways using the ruler and the embossing tool and fold over. Cut a 10 x 14½-cm (4 x 5½-in) rectangle from the bright yellow paper and glue it in the centre of the A4 folded card. Place the tag next. Line the thread up with the top right corner of the bright yellow rectangle and glue in place. Finally, position the second mounted daisy image from Step 5 in the centre, towards the bottom of the yellow rectangle and glue in place. ■

Beautiful butterflies

This is a lovely butterfly stamp and looks especially effective once coloured in and cut out. This card is given another dimension by cutting out the background, making the butterflies look as if they are almost fluttering out of the card.

YOU WILL NEED

A4 white card
Scissors
Ruler
Embossing tool

Black dye-based ink pad
Butterflies and flowers stamp
    7 x 7 cm (3 x 3 in)
Cutting mat

Craft knife
Felt tip pens in orange, yellow,
    blue, pink and black
3-D foam glue pads

1 Cut the A4 white card in half lengthways so that it is A5 in size. Score the A5 card down the centre lengthways using the ruler and the embossing tool and fold over. Lightly tap the black stamp pad onto the butterfly stamp to evenly cover it with ink. Stamp the image onto the front of the card, taking care not to rock the stamp during the process. Set aside to dry for a few minutes.

2 Open up the card, place it on the cutting mat and, using the craft knife, cut the detail from around the stamped image to create an aperture in the card. Take extra care when cutting around the delicate antennae of the butterfly. **steps 3–6 ▶**

3 Colour in the stamped image using the felt tip pens. An orange, yellow, blue and pink colour scheme has been used here but you can use whichever colours you prefer.

4 To give the coloured image a professional finish, colour along any exposed edges using a black felt tip pen. It is important you take care at this stage as you only want black felt pen along the edges of the aperture.

5 To create a three-dimensional effect, stamp the butterfly image twice more onto the remaining piece of white card and set aside to dry. Cut out around the flowers and butterflies of one of the stamped images and colour them in using the same colour scheme as in Step 3. Cut out one of the smaller flowers from the second stamped image which will be positioned at the top right hand corner of the card.

6 To assemble the card, apply 3-D foam glue pads to the back of the cut-out stamped butterflies and flowers. Remove the protective backing sheet from the foam pads and position each of the cut flower shapes over its corresponding shape on the card. Press them in position. Bend the butterflies' wings up slightly and apply 3-D foam glue pads to the back of the bodies then position them onto the card. Finally, glue the last flower on the top right hand corner of the white card. ■

Enamelled flower

The enamelled effect that is created for this card with the glamorous double embossing works best with simple stamp designs. Use as many coloured embossing powders as you like to achieve a bright and colourful effect.

Clear pigment ink pad
Piece of white paper
Daisy stamp 5 x 3 cm (2 x 1¼ in)
Embossing powders in pale green
    and lilac

Heat gun
Scissors
A5 pale green card
A5 lilac pearl card
A5 white card

A4 lilac card
Ruler
Embossing tool
Glue stick

1 To create a double embossed effect, rub the clear ink pad generously over a piece of white card large enough to hold the daisy stamp. While the ink is still wet, cover it with green embossing powder. Tap off the excess and return it to the pot. Holding the heat gun about 15 cm (6 in) away from the card, heat the embossing powder until it melts. Sprinkle the green embossing powder again over the hot melted powder. Tap off the excess and using the heat gun, heat the powder until it is hot. You will have to work quite quickly to achieve optimum results.

2 Repeat as in Step 1 but this time sprinkle the lilac embossing powder over half the area only. Adding another colour will give the final card a more pronounced enamelled effect. Take care not to scorch the card with the heat gun.

3 Take the daisy stamp and carefully stamp into the hot molten powder and hold the stamp down for about 20 seconds. Lift cleanly away, ensuring not to rock the stamp during the process. When cool, cut out the stamped image leaving a border around the flower.

4 Cut a 10 x 7½-cm (4 x 3-in) rectangle from the pale green card, a 8½ x 6-cm (3½ x 2½-in) rectangle from lilac pearl card and finally a 7 x 4½-cm (2½ x 1½-in) rectangle from the white card. Score the A4 lilac card down the centre lengthways using the ruler and the embossing tool and fold over. Mount all the layers of card and stamped image onto the front of the greeting card and glue in place. ■

Musical notes

Create this beautiful musical card for anyone with a love of music. Perfect if you have tried iris folding before as this is quite intricate, however, follow the simple instructions and you will soon master the technique.

YOU WILL NEED

A4 white card
Ruler
Embossing tool
4 sheets of A5 white paper
Craft knife
Cutting mat

Low tack masking tape
Pencil
A5 black paper
Scissors
Glue dots
Small musical note stamp

Black dye-based ink pad
A5 red paper
Sticky tape
Black fine-tipped marker pen

1 Score the A4 white card down the centre lengthways using the ruler and the embossing tool and fold over. Replicate the musical note template on page 126 onto a piece of A5 white paper. Hollow out the note using a craft knife. Place the hollowed out template on the front of the opened up A4 white card and secure it in place with low tack masking tape. Place the front of the card over the cutting mat and trace around the note with the pencil or the embossing tool. Remove the template and carefully cut around the tracing with the craft knife to make the aperture.

2 Position the A5 black paper on the back of the aperture so that it covers the top and legs of the musical note. You will have to cut around the base of the note, as shown above, and trim the sides of the black paper to allow the white card to fold over properly. Stick the black paper in place with glue dots. Turn the card over, place it on the cutting mat and cut away any black paper showing through at the base of the notes with the craft knife.
steps 3–6 ▶

3 Copy the iris folding template on page 126 onto another piece of A5 white paper. Position the hollowed out notes over the template, ensuring the card is wrong side up and secure in place with low tack masking tape.

4 Lightly tap the musical note stamp with the black ink pad and press it onto the A5 red paper, making sure not to rock the stamp. Re-ink as necessary and repeat until the surface of the paper is covered. Rotate the stamp so that the notes are random. Repeat onto one of the remaining A5 white paper. Once dry, cut out 2-cm ($^3/_4$-in) wide strips using the full length of the paper from both the red and white sheets. Fold the strips over lengthways ensuring the musical notes are on the outside.

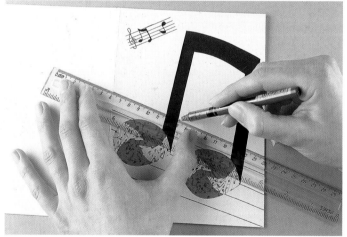

5 To begin iris folding, take a strip of the red stamped folded paper, lay the fold along the edge of Line 1 and secure in place with sticky tape. Next take a strip of the white stamped folded paper, lay the fold along Line 2 and secure in place with sticky tape. Complete the design by alternating the red and white stamped papers and sticking them down along the numbered lines.

6 Stick the last piece of A5 white paper over the back of the front card to make your card look neat. Turn the card over and using a black pen draw some lines so it looks like the musical notes are sitting on a score of music. In the top left hand corner draw five lines at an angle and a treble clef and two musical notes. You may wish to practise on a scrap of paper first. Be careful not to smudge the ink! ■

Frosty winter tree

This sophisticated card not only looks good, it's really simple to achieve. The combination of blues and silvers gives a beautiful finish. Anyone receiving this card would truly appreciate it.

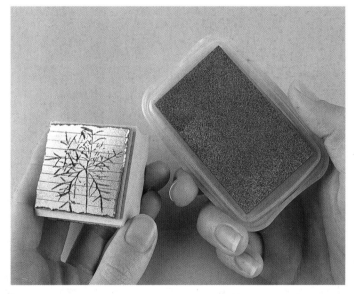

1 Lightly tap the top half of the winter tree stamp with the silver ink pad. Try not to get the ink on the edges of the stamp as this may spoil your stamped image.

2 Next, ink the lower half of the stamp with the sky blue ink pad. Stamp the image on a piece of white card large enough to hold the stamp, taking care not to rock the stamp during the process. Set aside to dry for a few minutes then cut around the image, leaving a small white border around the edge. **steps 3–6 ▶**

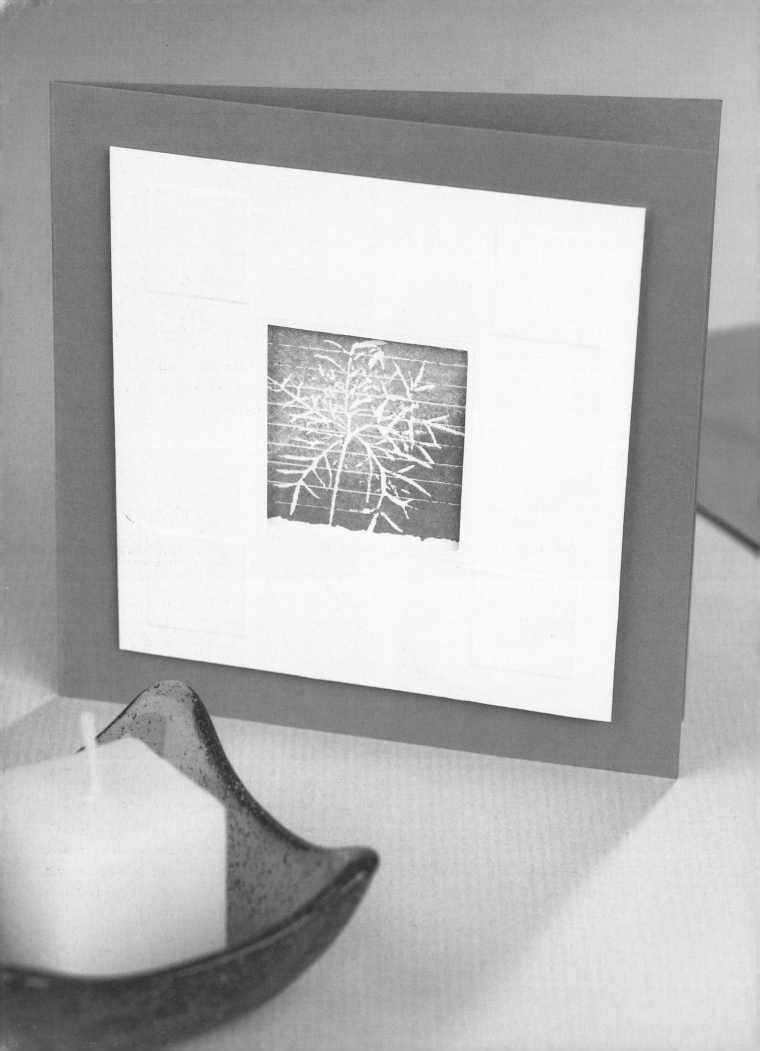

3 Cut an 11-cm (4$\frac{1}{2}$-in)square from the A5 white card. Place the square embossing template on the light box and secure it in place with low tack masking tape. Position the square card on the template and, using the embossing tool, trace out a square at each corner.

4 To create the aperture in the square card, measure a 4-cm (1$\frac{1}{2}$-in) square in the centre and cut it out over the cutting mat using a craft knife.

5 Cut out a 14 x 28-cm (5$\frac{1}{2}$ x 11-in) rectangle from the sky blue card. Score the card down the centre lengthways using the ruler and the embossing tool and fold over. Stick 3-D foam glue pads onto the front of the tree design around the white border.

6 Carefully lower the white aperture card from Step 4 over the tree design and when the design sits straight beneath the aperture, press it firmly down to stick it in place. Place a number of glue pads onto the back of the white card and stick it into place on the front of the sky blue card. ■

Balloons galore

Up, up and away with these beautiful balloons. Combine punches, stamping, matting and colouring to create this delightful design. Great as a party invitation or birthday card for someone with fun in their life.

YOU WILL NEED

Balloon punch
A5 purple card
A5 lilac card
A5 pink card
A4 cream pearl card
Ruler

Embossing tool
Pencil
Scissors
Craft knife
Cutting mat
Glue stick

Black dye-based ink pad
Balloon stamp 6 x 2½ cm (2½ x 1 in)
A5 cream card
Pink colouring pencil
3-D gloss

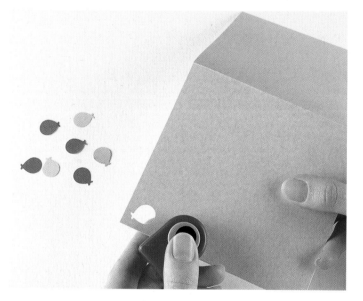

1 Using the balloon punch, punch out several balloon shapes out of the purple, lilac and pink cards. If you punch the balloons from a strip of paper, the piece that is left over can be used to decorate another card or as a stencil.

2 Cut the A4 cream pearl card to 13 x 26 cm (5 x 10 in). Score the card down the centre lengthways using the ruler and the embossing tool and fold over. Use the balloon punch to punch out a row of balloons along the front right edge of the card. **steps 3–7 ▶**

3 Cut out an 8 x 10-cm (3 x 4-in) rectangle from the purple card. Cut out a 7 x 9-cm (2½ x 3½-in) rectangle from the lilac card. Use a pair of scissors or a craft knife over the cutting mat to do this. Glue the purple rectangle onto the front of the cream pearl card, followed by the lilac rectangle over it.

4 Put some glue on part of the back of the purple and lilac balloons and position them so that they partly overlap the punched out balloon shapes on the cream pearl card.

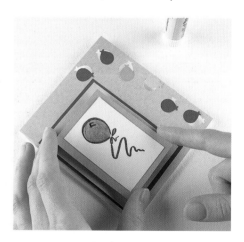

5 Lightly tap the black ink pad onto the balloon stamp and stamp the design onto a piece of cream card large enough to hold the stamp. Take care not to rock the stamp as this may smudge the design. Lift the stamp off cleanly. When dry, cut out around the balloon design so that it is 5 x 7 cm (2 x 2¾ in) in size. Colour in the balloon with a pink colouring pencil.

6 Apply 3-D gloss over the pink balloon, holding the bottle sideways over the image, and let the liquid run out on its own. Don't squeeze the bottle or you will get air bubbles. If you do get air bubbles pop them with a pin before the gloss dries. Set aside to dry for a few minutes.

7 Cut a 6 x 8 cm (2¼ x 3 in) rectangle from the pink card. To assemble the card, glue the design centrally over the pink. ■

Enamelled heart

Perfect for Valentine's day when you want to tell someone special you care. Try using several colours when embossing to create an enamelled look. Torn vellum looks better than regimented straight lines so experiment tearing scrap pieces of vellum to see how you get on.

YOU WILL NEED

Small piece of white card	Scissors	A5 white polka dot vellum
Gold pigment–based inkpad	A4 white card	A5 pale blue pearl card
Gold embossing powder	Ruler	Micro glue dots
Heat gun	Embossing tool	
Pencil	A5 light grey vellum	

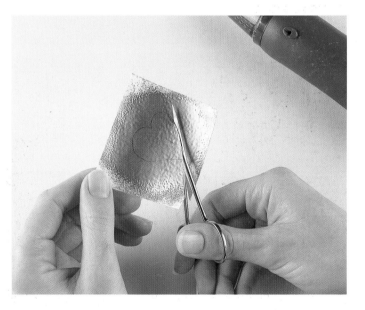

1 Wipe the gold inkpad over the surface of the small piece of white card. Sprinkle the gold embossing powder over the ink while it is still wet. Tap off the excess powder and return it to the pot. Hold the heat gun 15 cm (6 in) away from the card until the powder has melted. While the powder is still hot, sprinkle on some more powder and tap off the excess. Re-apply the heat to melt the second coat and repeat a third time.

2 When the gold enamelling has cooled slightly, pencil in a heart shape over it and cut it out using scissors.
steps 3–6 ▶

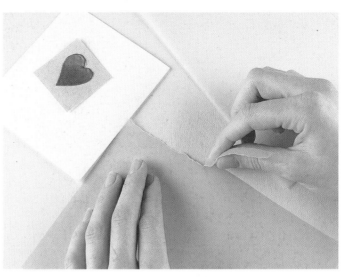

3 Place the heart onto a spare piece of card with the enamelled side uppermost. Hold the heat gun 15 cm (6 in) over the heart and apply the heat to the edges, being careful not to burn your design. Heat the heart until you can see the enamel begin to move.

4 Cut out a 12½ x 25-cm (5 x 10-in) rectangle from the A4 white card. Score the card down the centre lengthways using the ruler and the embossing tool and fold over. To tear the light grey vellum, hold it down firmly with one hand while gently tearing it with the other, as shown. Tear a 7-cm (3½-in) square.

5 From the white polka dot vellum, tear a 6-cm (2½-in) square. Cut a 5-cm (2-in) square from the pale blue pearl card. Stick the layers of vellum together rubbing on some micro glue dots onto the centre of each vellum layer so that they do not show through. Apply some micro glue dots to the back of the pearl pale blue card and stick this onto the centre of the vellums. Again using sticky dots, apply some to the centre of the pale blue vellum and stick this to the front of the white card.

6 To finish the card, apply micro glue dots to the back of the light grey vellum and fix it on the front of the card. Repeat the process with the polka dot vellum and position it in the middle of the grey vellum. Finally, apply micro glue dots to the back of the enamelled heart and position it in the centre of the baby blue square. ■

Sunflowers and butterflies

Sunflowers and butterflies are always popular. A lovely card for a birthday, get well or just thinking of you. Brighten someone's day with these merry and cheerful colours.

YOU WILL NEED

A4 cream card
Pencil
Craft knife
Cutting mat
Ruler
Embossing tool

Dye-based ink pads in green and black
Butterfly stamp 2½ x 2½ cm (1 x 1 in)
Flower in a vase stamp
   6 x 3 cm (2½ x 1¼ in)
Felt-tip pens in green, orange and yellow
Scissors

A5 yellow card
A 5 green card
Glue stick
3-D gloss
3-D foam glue pads

1 Cut out a 13 x 26-cm (5 x 10-in) rectangle from the A4 cream card using the craft knife and cutting mat. Score the card down the centre lengthways using the ruler and the embossing tool and fold over. Lightly tap the green ink pad over the butterfly stamp, ensuring the surface of the stamp is evenly coated. Stamp the design randomly onto the front of the card, re-inking as necessary and making sure not to rock the stamp during the process as this will smudge the design.

2 On the remaining cream card, stamp the butterfly design again, this time using the black ink pad. Now coat the flower in a vase stamp with the black ink pad and stamp the design onto the remaining cream card. When dry, colour in the butterfly and the flower design with green, orange and yellow felt tip pens – or your favourite colours. Cut around the butterfly, being extra careful around its delicate antennae. Cut out the flower in a vase design, leaving a small border around it. **steps 3–5** ▶

3 To assemble the layers, glue the flower design onto a piece of yellow card slightly larger than the card the flower is on. Stick the yellow card onto a piece of green card slightly larger than the yellow card.

4 Apply 3-D gloss over the flower design. Don't squeeze the bottle or you will get air bubbles. If you do get air bubbles pop them with a pin before the gloss dries. Set aside to dry for a few minutes.

5 To assemble the card, stick down the layers at an angle on the front of the cream card. Place a 3-D foam glue pad at the back of the butterfly and position it at the top right-hand corner of the card. ■

A dalliance with dragonflies

The long border stamp has a very stylish feel to it. I have stamped onto blue paper and used coloured pencils to colour in the image. Torn paper layered under the stamp completes the look for a quick and easy card that takes minutes to make.

YOU WILL NEED

A4 cream card
Ruler
Pencil
Scissors
Embossing tool
Dye-based ink pads in purple and black

Small dragonfly stamp
Dragonflies border stamp
A5 blue paper
Coloured pencils in pink, purple and lime green
Paintbrush

A5 purple card
Glue stick
3-D gloss

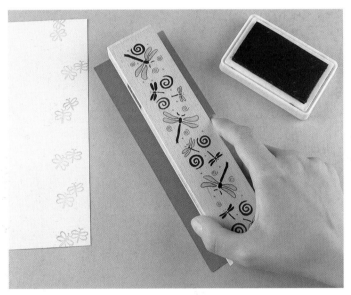

1 Cut a 20-cm (8-in) square from the A4 cream card. Score the card down the centre lengthways using the ruler and the embossing tool and fold over. Lightly tap the purple ink pad over the small dragonfly stamp and stamp a row of dragonflies down the front right-hand side of the card, re-inking as necessary. Take care not to rock the stamp during the process as this will smudge the design.

2 Lightly tap the black ink pad over the dragonflies border stamp and position it over a strip of blue paper long enough to hold the design, applying even pressure along the length of the stamp. You may want to practise on a scrap piece of paper first. Set aside to dry for a few minutes. **steps 3–6 ▶**

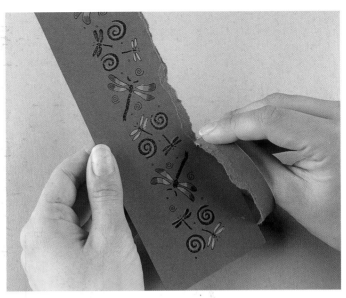

3 Colour in the dragonflies using a selection of coloured pencils. Trace colour around the swirls on the design to create a shadow effect.

4 Place the ruler along the length of the stamped dragonfly image and run a clean wet paintbrush along the edge of the ruler to soften the paper. Carefully tear the paper away. Repeat on all three remaining sides.

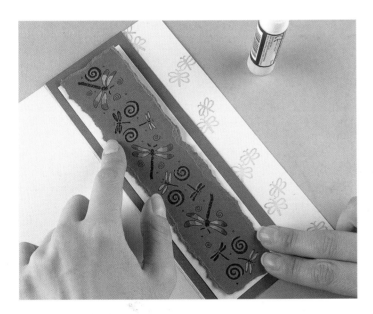

5 Cut a rectangle of cream card slightly larger than the torn blue paper. Next, cut a piece of purple card slightly larger than the cream paper. Stick the layers together, with the largest at the bottom and position onto the front of the stamped cream card.

6 Finally, apply 3-D gloss to the dragonflies, taking care not to squeeze the bottle when applying it as this will create air bubbles. If you do get air bubbles, pop them with a pin before the gloss dries. Set aside to dry for a few minutes. ■

Templates

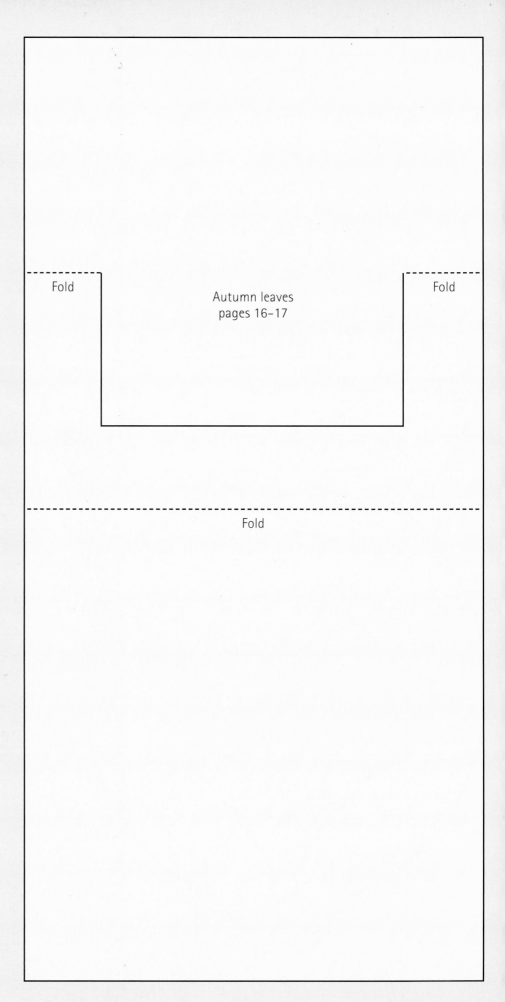

Fold

Autumn leaves
pages 16–17

Fold

Fold

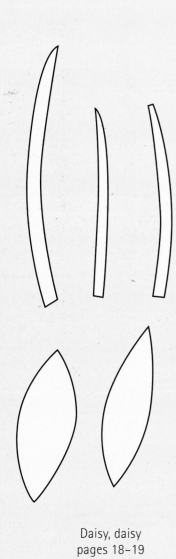

Daisy, daisy
pages 18–19

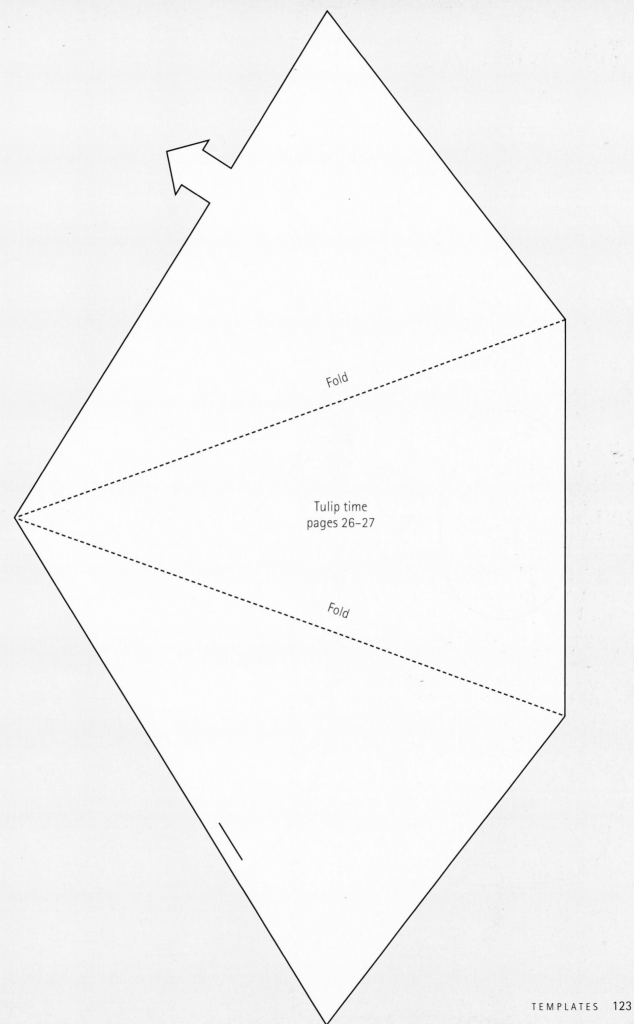

Fold

Tulip time
pages 26–27

Fold

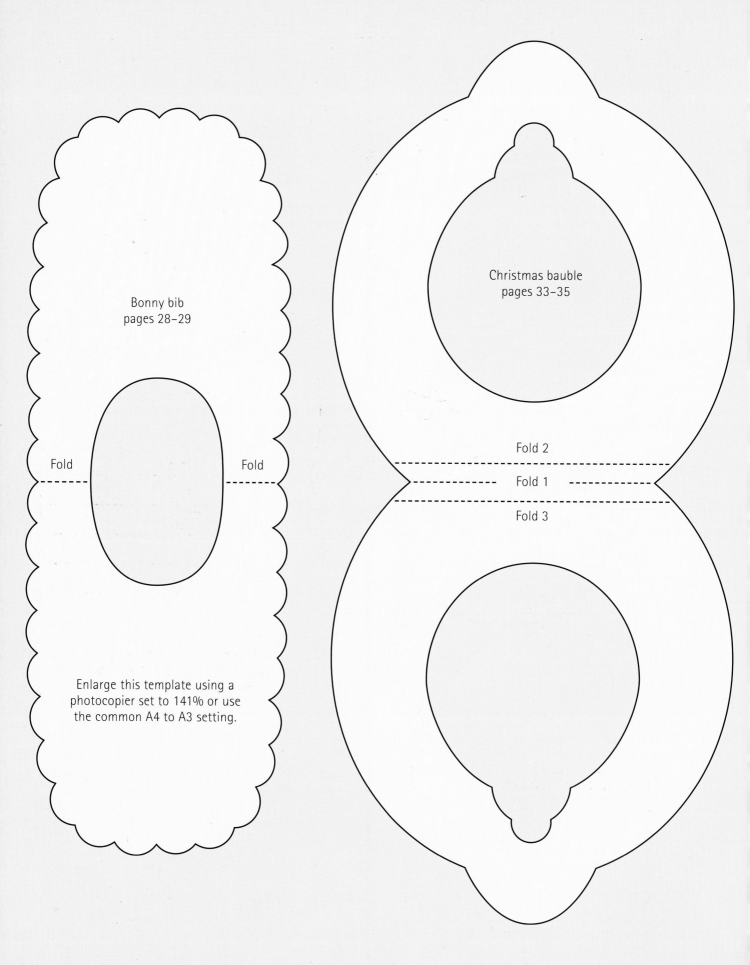

Bonny bib
pages 28–29

Fold

Fold

Enlarge this template using a
photocopier set to 141% or use
the common A4 to A3 setting.

Christmas bauble
pages 33–35

Fold 2

Fold 1

Fold 3

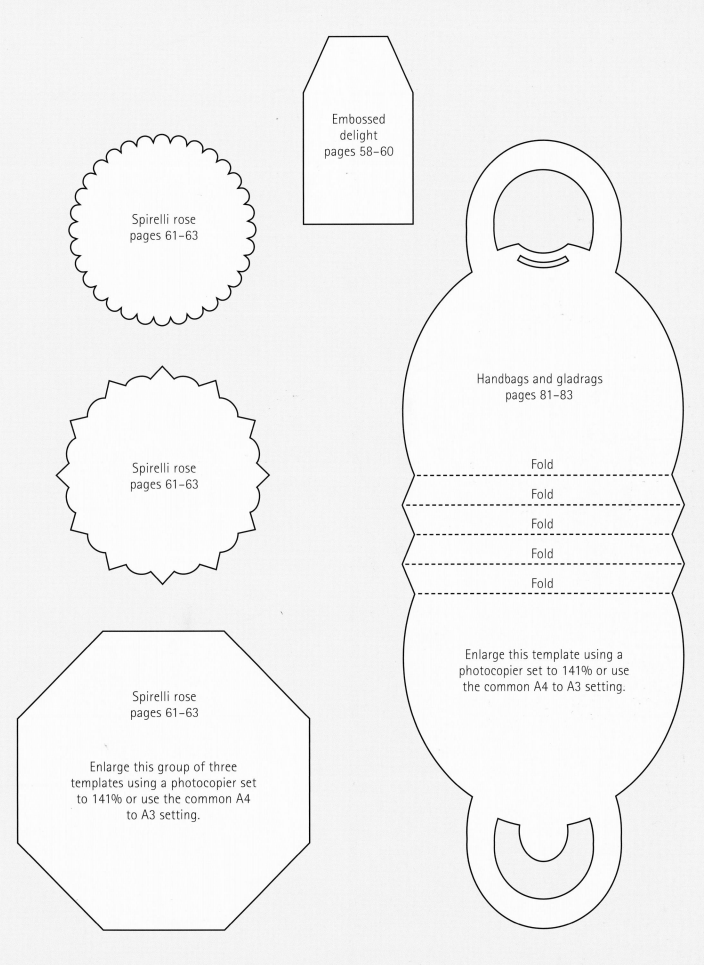

Embossed
delight
pages 58–60

Spirelli rose
pages 61–63

Spirelli rose
pages 61–63

Handbags and gladrags
pages 81–83

Fold

Fold

Fold

Fold

Fold

Spirelli rose
pages 61–63

Enlarge this group of three
templates using a photocopier set
to 141% or use the common A4
to A3 setting.

Enlarge this template using a
photocopier set to 141% or use
the common A4 to A3 setting.

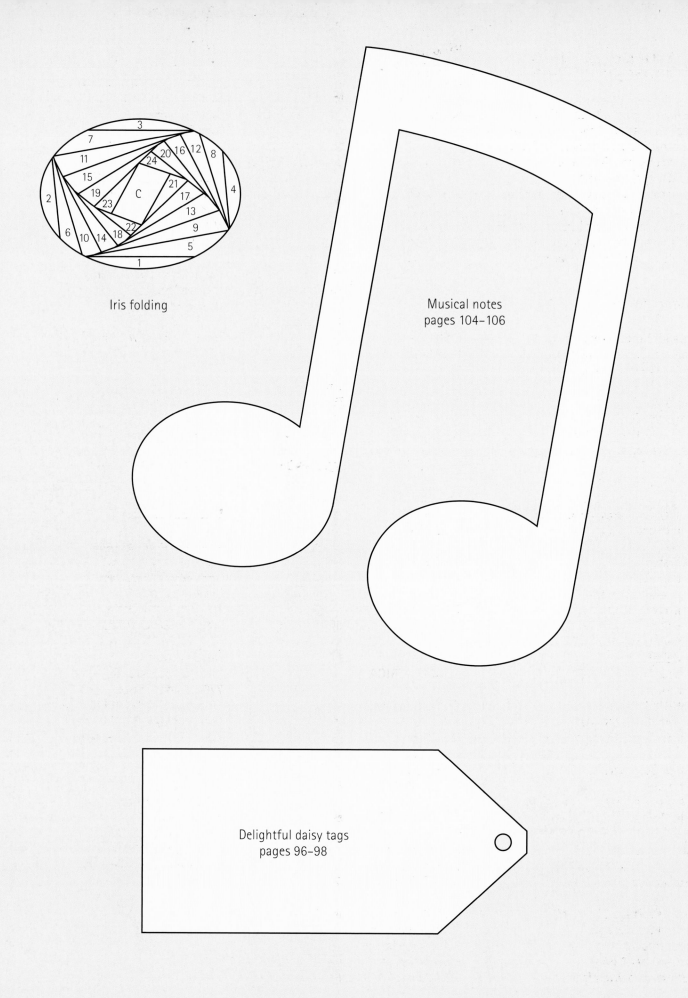

Iris folding

Musical notes
pages 104–106

Delightful daisy tags
pages 96–98

Suppliers

The following list of companies are suppliers of some of the products used in this book. The page numbers in brackets refer to projects that contain materials available from that particular supplier. Your local craft shop will also stock a good range of stencils, stickers and stamps. Some are suppliers to the trade only. Contact the company or visit the website for a full list of retail stockists.

UNITED KINGDOM

Art and Crafts Direct (pp 18, 42)
(mail order/general craft suppliers)
Unit 44 Coney Green Business Park
Wingfield View
Clay Cross
Derbyshire S45 9JW
Tel: +44 (0)1246 252313
Web: www.artandcraftsdirect.com

Artoz (pp 16, 26, 28)
(stickers and general paper suppliers)
Tannery Court Business Centre
Knight Road
Strood
Rochester
Kent ME2 2JH
Tel: + 44 (0)1634 722060
Web: www.artoz.co.uk

Clarity Stamps
Ludwells Farm
Spode Lane
Cowden
Kent TN8 7HN
Tel: +44 (0)1342 850111
Web: www.claritystamp.co.uk

Design Objectives (p 45)
(trade supplier)
4–8 Fleets Industrial Estate
Willis Way
Poole
Dorset BH15 3SU
Tel: +44 (0)1202 679976
Web: www.docrafts.co.uk

Hobby Craft (pp 36, 39, 45)
(general craft supplier)
Stores throughout the UK
Tel: 0800 027 3387
Web: www.hobbycraft.co.uk

Personal Impressions
(trade suppliers)
Curzon Road
Chilton Industrial estate
Sudbury
Suffolk CO10 2XW
Tel: +44 (0)1787 375241
Web: www.richstamp.co.uk (for stockists)

Trim Craft (p 30)
Basford Works
Egypt Road
New Basford
Nottingham NG7 7GD
Tel: +44 (0)115 9787899
Web: www.trimcraft.co.uk (for stockists)

Viking Industrial Products Ltd (p 23)
Unit 1 Coronation Business Park
Hard Ings Road
Keighley
West Yorkshire BD21 3ND
Tel: +44 (0)1535 610373
Web: www.vikingtapes.co.uk

HOLLAND/GERMANY/FRANCE

Kars and CO BV (pp 20, 33)
(craft suppliers)
Industrieweg 27
Industriesterrein De Heuning
Postbus 97
4050 EB Ochten
Holland
Tel: +31 344642864
Web: www.kars.nl (retail stockists)

SOUTH AFRICA

Crafty Supplies
Shop UG 104 The Atrium
Main Road
Claremont
Cape Town
Tel: +27 (0)21 671 0286

Art Crafts and Hobbies
72 Hibernia Street
PO Box 9635
George 6530
Tel: +27 (0)44 874 1337

**L&P Stationery and Artists
   Requirements**
65b Church Street
Bloemfontein
Tel: +27 (0)51 430 1085

AUSTRALIA

Anderson Arts and Crafts
64-68 Violet Street
Revesby
NSW 2212
Tel: +61 (0)20 9772 1066

Edgeworth Craft supplies
63 Edgeworth David Avenue
Waitara
NSW
Tel: +61 (0)20 9489 3909

Craft Warehouse Shop
Campbell Street
Bowen Hills
QLD 4006
Tel: +61 (0)7 3257 1739

Lincraft
Gallery Level
Imperial Arcade
Pitt Street
Sydney
NSW 2000
Tel: +61 (0)20 9221 5111

UNITED STATES

Michaels Arts and Crafts
(general craft supplier)
8000 Bent Branch Drive
Irving, TX 75063
Tel: +1 (214) 4091300
Web: www.michaels.com

Hobby Lobby
(general craft supplier)
7707 SW 44th Street
Oklahoma City, OK 73179
Tel: +1 (405) 7451100
Web: www.hobbylobby.com

Plaid
(trade supplier)
3225 Westech Drive
Norcross
Georgia 3009-23500
Tel: +1 (678) 2918100
Web: www.plaidonline.com

Index